.

SCIOTO COUNTY'S WAR WITH SPAIN

SCIOTO COUNTY'S WAR WITH SPAIN

JOHN McHENRY

THE
History
PRESS

Published by The History Press
Charleston, SC
www.historypress.com

Front cover: Four of the five Company H members who died during their deployment. *From left to right*: Henry M. Morrison, Elbert Patterson, Daniel Dodge and Forrest Briggs. Not pictured is Kurt Sparks from Columbus, who joined when the unit was at Camp Bushnell.

First published 2021

ISBN 9781540246578

Library of Congress Control Number: 2020948438

For all those before,
now and after.

CONTENTS

CONTENTS

FOREWORD

At the start of the Spanish-American War, in April 1898, men from Portsmouth and Scioto County rallied to the cause of the Cuban independence movement. While the majority of U.S. infantry troops deployed in the war served in Cuba and participated in its occupation, men from Company H (Portsmouth, Ohio) found themselves among the more than nine thousand troops sent to Puerto Rico, participating in the U.S. invasion and occupation of this neighboring Spanish Caribbean colony. The men of Company H and the Fourteenth OVI were generally welcomed as liberators—armed forces who were there to evict Puerto Rico's oppressive Spanish colonizers.

Thanks to John McHenry's research and telling, we now have a detailed account of Company H's role in the Spanish-American War, a conflict that launched the United States on the path to becoming a world power, one with its own colonial possessions in the Caribbean and Pacific. In the larger scheme of imperial expansion, Company H and other Scioto Countians played their part in the ultimate annexation of Puerto Rico by the United States.

Overshadowed by the wars that followed—World War I and World War II—the story of Company H and Scioto county's "invasion of Puerto Rico" has, for many years, laid sleeping in the columns of Charles Hard's *Portsmouth Blade* and J.L. Patterson's *Portsmouth Daily Times*. As a local analog of the era's more widely known contest between the papers of Pulitzer and Hearst, local press championed the U.S. cause in general and heaped praise on the valor and heroism of Company H's regular soldiers. Hard and Patterson, however, disagreed over the merits of the unit's officer corps, but their editorial clashes, in the end, appeared more partisan than personal.

References to the men of Company H and the "Spanish War" can be found in the memorial landscape of Scioto County and Puerto Rico. In southern Ohio, on the banks of Turkey Creek in the Shawnee State Forest, an obscure and overlooked historical plaque can be located on a flagpole on the parade grounds of Boy Scout Camp Oyo. A more substantial and prominent memorial—and one that is largely inaccessible to Scioto Countians today—can be found in the village square of Guayama, Puerto Rico, located six miles inland from the southern coastal port of Arroyo, where the Fourth OVI and Company H first came ashore in their campaign against Spain in August 1898. There, a traveler can find "a memorial plaque affixed to a concrete block," on which the names of the Scioto County men "who lost their lives in the performance of their duty in the war with Spain" are immortalized.

With this book, those men who died in the war and all of their brothers in arms from Company H specifically and Scioto County generally— those men who made it safely back to Scioto County—have now been memorialized in print, their history accessible to all.

—Andrew Lee Feight, PhD,
Shawnee State University, Portsmouth, Ohio

PREFACE

Clarence Clark was from Harrison Township, Scioto County, Ohio. He was not famous or well-known beyond his family and friends. His life was, however, notable for one consequence. At what we can assume was an early age, he left Harrison Township and went to the Denver, Colorado area to find what we can assume again was his fortune. He must have been a rather adventurous type, as, at some point, it was reported that, while there, he joined the First Volunteer Calvary, better known as Teddy Roosevelt's Rough Riders. That famous military unit made its name in the Spanish-American War waged in Cuba. Perhaps young Clark from Harrison Township fought with Roosevelt there. Perhaps he charged up one of those hills, or maybe he was wounded. Maybe he came down with yellow fever or typhoid like so many other soldiers. Or maybe he was not there at all and never was a trooper with the Rough Riders. The newspaper the *Portsmouth Blade* reported in its June 29, 1898 edition the enlistment of Clarence Clark with the Rough Riders and that he was in the Battle of Santiago, but his name does not appear on the unit roster. It is also not known if anyone named Clarence Clark from Harrison Township found his fortune in Colorado. But then, in the July 1, 1898 edition of the rival newspaper, the *Daily Times*, it was reported that Clarence Clark, who was born and raised in Harrisonville and was the cousin of the street railway conductor John McCurdy, joined a western regiment of Rough Riders in Colorado and was shipped out to Manila, Philippines. The simple fact here is that there were no Rough Riders in the Philippines.

Making local history even murkier, the July 7, 1898 edition of *the Portsmouth Blade* reported that a certain Edward Lauterbach from Harrison Township joined the Rough Riders when he was in Texas and was in Troop B. Again, as with Clarence Clark, his name is not on the Rough Riders' roster. Such are the twists and turns of historical research. Perhaps with a little more shuffling through papers and documents or cracking open moldy books, our Clarence Clark and Edward Lauterbach will allow themselves to be discovered. Undeniable though is the fact that when war with Spain was declared, Scioto County, Ohio, rallied around the flag. Today, the men and one woman of Scioto County, and the war they fought, are all but forgotten.

If any one of us were asked about Scioto County and Portsmouth in relation to war, we would probably cite the Civil War, World War I, World War II, Korea, Vietnam or any of our "modern wars." The Cold War might even pop up. But it is a safe bet that the Spanish-American War would not make the list.

This book pays tribute to those men—and one woman—from Scioto County, Ohio, who participated in the Spanish-American War. As American wars go, this one was short. The United States declared war on Spain on April 25, 1898, and officially ended it by signing the Treaty of Paris on December 10, 1898. The fighting had already ceased in the Caribbean theater in August.

Like the rest of the country at the tail end of the nineteenth century, the people of Scioto County, Ohio, lived their daily lives adjusting to change. The country had weathered the depression of 1893, complete with a Wall Street panic; the failure of the Reading Railroad; millions unemployed; and the march on the nation's capital of Coxey's Army demanding work.[1] From that upheaval came the utter defeat of the Democrats in the Congressional elections of 1894 and the election of William McKinley to the presidency in 1896. The nation's economy started to mend, boosted by dramatic changes in transportation, communication, industry and agriculture. Add to the mix a resounding victory over Spain in "a splendid little war" and America found itself with a world empire on the cusp of the "American Century."[2] Willing or not, the people of Scioto County and Portsmouth and their soldier boys were there for the ride.

The easiest story to tell is that of Company H, Fourteenth Ohio Volunteer Infantry.[3] Made up almost exclusively of men from Portsmouth and Scioto County, the official roster of this national guard unit rings with names familiar to us today: Kinney, Davis, Calvert, Funk, Reinhardt, Shela, Patterson,

Pictured are some of the Company H soldiers, most likely before their departure as suggested by their hats. Notice the African American man in the background on the far right who appears to be holding a bag. At that time, military units were segregated, so he was most likely attached as a steward or cook. *Courtesy of the Southern Ohio Museum and Cultural Center, Portsmouth, Ohio.*

Herms, Distel, Dodge, Searl, Foster and Noel. Others are probably not so familiar, their family names having faded from local history: Trimmer, McGuire, Zeek, Crouse and Winters (Appendix A). Altogether—recognizable or not—seventy-four men marched down Second Street one warm April day, assembled on Government Square (now the Esplanade) for some encouraging words and then made their way to the N&W train waiting for them at the station at the corner of Tenth and Waller Streets.

Then there is the harder story to tell, that of those from Scioto County who answered the call but were not in Company H (Appendix B). They were scattered around in other units—some in national guard units and others in the United States Army and Navy. These were perhaps young men, like Clarence Clark and Edward Lauterbach from Harrison Township. To the extent possible, this book honors them all—both the known and unknown.

Acknowledgements

For people like me who enjoy delving into local history, the Portsmouth Public Library is a gold mine. For a while, I lived in the Local History Room, surrounded by Carolyn Cottrell and her courteous staff. They greet everyone who enters the room and asks how they can help. It is an amazing resource. Director Paige Williams is the overall guiding light.

I also want to acknowledge the suggestions and input of Larry Strayer, a collector extraordinaire of military photographs and artifacts. Many of his photographs appear in books about the Civil War. Larry has taken an interest in the Fourth Ohio Volunteer Infantry and actually has a uniform from a Company H soldier, Joseph C. Bratt.

My thanks is also extended to Major (Ret.) Mark S. Ballard for his research of the National Archives for me. He is the director of the research division of Militree Branches Genealogical Research, 5655 Hawk Lake Drive, Fulton, Missouri, 65251. Mark is retired from the Ohio National Guard.

The Scioto County Probate Court in Portsmouth, Ohio, has some limited records of births and deaths. Director Pam Hutchinson and her friendly staff provide excellent guidance.

The library of the Ohio Historical Connection, located at 800 East Seventeenth Avenue, Columbus, Ohio, 43211, is a required visit for anyone plunging into any facet of Ohio history. I found the staff there very willing to tutor this neophyte.

I particularly want to thank John Rodrigue and Ashley Hill of The History Press, whose guidance was invaluable. This book would not have happened without them.

NOTE TO THE READER

This book mostly uses the contemporary spelling of Puerto Rico. When citing writings of the time (circa 1898), spelling using *o* in place of *ue* is preserved. Hence, "Porto Rico."

In 1911, the addresses in Portsmouth were changed. Addresses in this book predate that change. One can find the post-1911 addresses on the Sanborn Fire Insurance Map of Portsmouth that is available from the Library of Congress.

1

BEGINNING

I f you had been a young man living in Scioto County, Ohio, on New Year's Eve in 1897, you would have had your pick of twenty-eight barbershops and nine menswear clothing stores to help you prepare for the reverie you could find in any of the fifty-two saloons that were scattered about the city of Portsmouth, the largest city on the Ohio River between Cincinnati and Marietta. And you could buy your celebratory cigar at any of the city's sixteen tobacco shops. Not mentioned in the City Directory of Portsmouth and Scioto County of August 1897 but described in the *Daily Times* was the Eleventh Street "Resort" of Jennie Matthews, the "dove nest" where "eight little birdies" worked. One can assume that the next day's police arrest records suggested a brisk trade in all the pleasure places of the city. Arrestees had their pick of thirty-seven attorneys to help them out of their overly exuberant New Year's Eve celebrations. The diaries of Captain William Moore and that of his daughter Louisiana reported rather mild winter weather then.

Not everyone indulged themselves with saloons and other diversions. There were as many as sixteen churches in the city alone, and there were undoubtedly many in the county to guide the pious into the next year. Or, if you preferred, you might just hitch your team to the old family buggy and go ring in the new year with relatives and friends. The four carriage shops and five harness and horse tack outlets in the city were there to service your personal transportation needs.

Contemporary publications inflamed the public's passions and romanticized the war.
Courtesy of the Library of Congress.

Portsmouth was thriving in the last half of the 1890s. It saw its population increase from 12,394 in 1890 to 17,870 in 1900. The county overall saw a jump from 35,377 to 40,981. Portsmouth and Scioto County were up and coming, pulled along with the rest of the country in the economic recovery from the depression of 1893.

The first run of the Portsmouth Street Railroad and Light Company kicked off in 1893 with a route to New Boston. It could transport twenty-four people at a time, taking them to their jobs and various visitations. The line was eventually expanded to include stops in Sciotoville, Wheelersburg, Franklin Furnace and even Ironton in neighboring Lawrence County. A common form of entertainment was spending the day on an excursion from Portsmouth to wherever there was a stop and back again.

In 1898, the largest fire to date destroyed the Burgess Steel Mill located at Front and Washington Streets. The effort to rebuild was led by the owner, Levi York, a mover and shaker in many community projects. In 1899, he began rebuilding his steel mill in New Boston. Alongside it, a park complex called Millbrook Park took shape. When completed, residents could take the "Street Railroad" to the park, where they could enjoy a rollercoaster, a

Pictured is part of Millbrook Park in New Boston. Levi York added the park to the construction of his steel mill when he relocated it from Portsmouth after it was destroyed by a fire in 1898. Returning veterans of the Spanish-American War undoubtedly enjoyed the many attractions of the park. *Courtesy of the Southern Ohio Museum and Cultural Center, Portsmouth, Ohio.*

casino, a baseball stadium and a dancing and skating pavilion and then top off their day with a leisurely boat ride on the lake. The returning veterans of the Spanish-American War certainly strolled along the tree-lined walkways with family, friends and sweethearts and joined in the various amusements.

In 1897, the Enos Reed Pharmacy, located at 601 Second Street, was the first business in the town to sell Coca-Cola.[4] Shoe manufactures, brickyards and the steel mill were booming. During the 1890s, nine newspapers were circulated; one of them was even printed in German. Great things were happening in the city at the confluence of the mighty Scioto and Ohio Rivers. In 1898, many of the young men working in the city's shoe factories, brickyards, farms and steel mill found themselves a thousand miles away from cold, temperate southern Ohio and in tropical Puerto Rico before the year ended.

An 1896 picture of Scioto County youth at camp. Some appear to have weapons. R. Stanley Pritchard (*standing to the left*) was later the Captain of Company H when it departed Portsmouth. He was relieved of his command before leaving for Puerto Rico. *Courtesy of the Southern Ohio Museum and Cultural Center, Portsmouth, Ohio.*

(*Reverse of the image above*) Two years later, Alger and McGuire found themselves in Puerto Rico. *Courtesy of the Southern Ohio Museum and Cultural Center, Portsmouth, Ohio.*

Of course, nothing is ever perfect; not everything in the city and county was fine. Newspapers and gossip were the sole carriers of information— good, bad, modest and salacious. Even with the advent of the "Street Railroad," horses were still the typical mode of transportation in the county, resulting in sanitation issues. If a horse died in the middle of the street, removal became a burdensome undertaking. Obituaries often reported cases of diphtheria, cholera and pneumonia. Numerous accidents maimed and killed the town's residents. The city engineer at the time, B.C. Bratt, struggled with an inadequate sewage system. Fires were common. The horse-drawn pumpers were inadequate for all but the most modest of fires. A common practice in firefighting was to save the adjacent structures and let the stricken one burn down. A few weeks after Company H took the train out of Portsmouth, a fire destroyed eleven homes and businesses that were bound by Second and Front Streets to the north and south and Market and Court Streets to the east and west. Company H had marched by these buildings on its way to the train station. Then came the then largest fire in city's history; on June 7, 1898, the Burgess Steel and Ironworks burned down. Five hundred men were thrown out of work.

Seasonal floods came right on time every March. The rivers and streams sent folks to higher ground, and when the water receded, the residents were left to sort through the debris and recover. The aggravation of rising water wasn't so bad in 1898. The March 30, 1898 edition of the *Portsmouth Blade* reported that the Ohio River only rose to the sidewalk by the Biggs House, located on the corner of Market and Front Streets. The newspaper credited Mayor Charles Glidden and City Engineer B.C. Bratt for installing a system of pumps and dikes that held back the water from Third Street. Everyone was relieved that things weren't as bad as they were after the flood of 1884, which was, at that time, the worst flood in the city's history.

All in all, the good people of Scioto County, Ohio, in 1898 were the same as they are today. They talked about politics and read the papers, and they took sides. The *Portsmouth Blade* was strictly Republican, while its rival, the *Portsmouth Daily Times*, was Democratic. In addition to pointing their acerbic pens at each other and unashamedly throwing insults, they reported on murder trials, divorces, fights, thefts, foreclosures and the sheriff's sales of property. New businesses tried to make it, but most did not. Large print advertisements for clothing and shoes grabbed readers' eyes. Smaller print was used for advertising lumber and garden seeds. Attorneys, dentists, physicians, pharmacists, insurance agents and saddle and harness makers also announced themselves in the papers. The newspapers were notorious

Charles E. Hard (*right*), the editor of the *Portsmouth Blade*, and J.L. Patterson (*above*), the editor of the *Daily Times*, were fierce competitors who had no hesitation when attacking each other personally. *Courtesy of the Portsmouth Public Library, Portsmouth, Ohio.*

HON. CHAS. E. HARD,
EDITOR
"THE DAILY BLADE."
POST MASTER.

for gossip. The droll reports of mundane life must have captivated readers, like Facebook today. The following report was typical:

So far, nothing has been heard of the packages stolen from Batterson's buggy in the alley near Lake's stable. People should be more careful about leaving packages in their buggies.

Mrs. Frank Pratt is very ill with rheumatism at her home on East Fourth Street.

Ben Davis was in Maysville, Sunday, visiting relatives.

There was a fine little scrap at the South Side Depot Friday. Joe Shurer, a wagon driver, got into an argument with George Clovin, baggage handler at the depot. Clovin hit Shurer, and the latter's head hit the platform. By the time Shurer had been brought to his senses, the referee had given the decision to Clovin.

And this gem:

> *Eli Neff has the record, catching five opossum, eight skunks and six coons in one night.*

So, as it was then, so it is now. Life was hard for some, not bad for others and very easy for a few. The births and deaths of people and their dreams made the essence of their lives—and they talked of war.

SETTING THE STAGE FOR WAR

C uban exertions for independence from Spain broke into armed rebellion in 1868 with what became known as the Ten Years' War. American sympathizers began advocating for the rebels; war bonds were actually sold in the United States to raise money to support their fight.

Then, on October 30, 1873, came the *Virginius* incident. An American named John Patterson, in sympathy with the Cuban insurgents, purchased the old steamer *Virginius* from the government; it had originally been captured from the Confederacy during the Civil War. For three years, Patterson used the steamer to transport men and war materials to the rebels. Then, the boat's good luck of running blockades ran out. The *Virginius* was captured, and its captain, Joseph Fry, crew of 52 and 103 Cuban rebels were hauled into Santiago, Cuba. Beginning the day after a bogus trial, 53 of the captives were executed, including Captain Fry and some American crew members. The vigorous diplomatic efforts made by the United States and Britain, including a threat of war, prevented other executions. The remaining prisoners and the *Virginius* were turned over to the U.S. Navy. Spain eventually paid $80,000 worth of reparations to the families of the executed Americans.

The *Virginius*'s dust-up with Spain became a call for war. War cries and exhortations for revenge raged from newspapers and politicians. The fever burned hot and then cooled down. After all, only eight years had passed since the horror of the Civil War. The president at the time, Ulysses S. Grant, had seen enough of war and was not about to get the country into another one. He had his hands full with Reconstruction in the South and corruption scandals in his administration. In 1876, the nation had its attention turned toward the centennial of its birth, Custer's defeat at Little Big Horn and a red-hot presidential campaign that saw, for the second time in American history, the winner of the popular vote, Samuel Tilden, lose the presidency to the electoral college winner, Rutherford Hayes.

Still, the *Virginius* had primed the pump. At the end of the Ten Years' War, there were Cubans who felt the struggle had accomplished nothing. For them, embers still glowed for Cuban independence. The American outrage over the *Virginius*—though it had mostly petered out—told Cubans that Americans could identify with their struggle for freedom. The Cubans' want for guns, ammunition, supplies and iron was the only thing that kept the island from freedom. Some of those Cubans went to New York in search of compatriots who would support the island's continuing struggle with money and promotion to the public. They found a ready audience in Cuban émigrés and some passionate Americans. By 1892, like-minded radicals had coalesced into a formal movement—the Cuban Revolutionary Party. By 1896, a Cuban-American Fair had opened in New York. Cuban support clubs and rallies started popping up around the country. Cincinnati, Akron and Cleveland were among the ranks of host cities. With a secret party cell set up in Havana and the creation of a militant wing, it was only a matter of time before a second insurgency began—the questions became when and how. The answer came in 1895, when six revolutionaries slipped ashore—onto the soil of their homeland—at night. The second fight for Cuban independence began.

The *Virginius* matter made the U.S. Navy look long and hard at itself. It concluded that it would need to build a modern fleet of steel ships. Gone were the days of sails and side-wheeled steamers. Coal-fired battleships, cruisers and modern-styled monitors were launched from shipyards. It became a formidable force that included the cruisers USS *Cincinnati* and USS *Brooklyn* and the battleships USS *Oregon*, USS *Olympia* and USS *Maine*.

The United States Army was a different story. Apparently, the impression of the War Department was that the naval spat with Spain mattered little to the army. The sense of urgency that seeped into the navy after the *Virginius* incident had no effect on the War Department. Tasked solely with the operation of the United States Army, its ten separate bureaus lumbered along. At the outbreak of war in 1898, the army had 28,747 officers and enlisted men scattered along coastal defenses to the Rio Grande border.

Tending to some of the wounded—probably in Cuba, where most of the fighting occurred. *From the Library of Congress.*

When war broke out with Spain, the administrative management of the army's operations in the Caribbean became a national scandal. Everything, large and small, had a glitch. The rations were foul. The uniforms were woolen and hot. The rifles were outdated. Inadequate camp sanitation bred disease. The camps' medical care facilities were short on supplies and physicians. In the prosecution of the Spanish-American War, the United States Navy outshined the United States Army.

The American agitation with Spain gained momentum. While the government under President Grover Cleveland tried to steer a neutral course, politicians, newspapers and organizations, such as the Civil War Veterans of the Grand Army of the Republic (GAR), kept beating the war drum. On March 8, 1895, when an intemperate Spanish gunboat captain fired on an American merchant ship, the newspapers went airborne. From then on, rivers of ink flowed about the outrages that Spain had heaped on the United States and its flag. The public's sympathy with the Cuban rebels began to move toward militancy against Spain. The United States began pushing Spain to abandon Cuba, its "Ever Faithful Isle." The navy thought it prudent to station a warship at Key West, just in case it was necessary to steam into Havana Harbor with a landing force. The USS *Maine* was dispatched.

NEW YORK HERALD, SUNDAY, APRIL 10, 1898.

OUR MODERN DON QUIXOTE.

Contemporary publications inflamed the public's passions and romanticized the war. *From the Library of Congress.*

And this is how it was for the next few years, when, after all the bellicosity and snarling between the United States and Spain, the latter agreed to grant Cuba and Puerto Rico limited autonomy effective on January 1, 1898. The American public's support was mixed. The new president, William McKinley, and a few American newspapers wanted to give Cuban and Puerto Rican autonomy a chance, but many other newspapers did not. These newspapers had a field day reporting on the food shortages and deplorable housing conditions in Cuba. It reached "fake news" levels, with William Randolph Hearst of the *New York Journal* blatantly falsifying that riots were aimed against Americans. Clearly, it was time for an American warship to pay a "courtesy" call to the island. So, the USS *Maine*, with 343

Contemporary publications inflamed the public's passions and romanticized the war. *From the Library of Congress.*

enlisted and 31 officers, set sail from Key West and steamed into Havana Harbor on January 25, 1898.

For the next three weeks, the relationship between the USS *Maine* and Havana was courteous. The USS *Maine* stayed quietly moored in Havana Harbor, taking on Spanish sightseers. There was, however, a diplomatic explosion involving a letter penned by the Spanish minister to the United States calling McKinley a "cheap politician." The howl went up. Such a cheap insult could not be ignored. All the old wounds and insults came back to life. Courteous diplomacy fractured wide open. So, on the evening of February 15, 1898, just as the bugler finished taps, the USS *Maine* was blown to smithereens, killing 260 American sailors. Spain was blamed, and the stage was set for war.[5]

3

ROUSING FOR WAR

The people of Scioto County, Ohio, knew what was going on. The Portsmouth newspapers reported on Cuban business. Even the *Virginius* episode was given ink. The November 22, 1873 edition of the *Portsmouth Times* opined about "recent outrages" and the heroics of the Cuban "struggling patriots." At one time or another, the nine Portsmouth newspapers of that era gave space to Cuba and Spain. As diplomatic blusters increased, so did reports on Spanish atrocities—both real and exaggerated. The next edition of the *Portsmouth Blade*, after the New Year's Eve celebration, reported on the movement of Spanish troops meant to relieve Santa Cruz under attack from rebels. The election of Frank Pratt Jr. to first lieutenant of Company H was also reported. Pratt's efforts to gain a promotion were announced in the characteristically chatty style of that era's newspaper reporting.

Co. H. Election
Frank Pratt Jr. Selected as First Lieutenant of the Company

The election for first lieutenant of Co. H. held at the armory last night did not result to the satisfaction of those in authority. The contesting candidates were J.A. Smith, the contracting carpenter, and Frank Pratt, the paper hanger. Smith was the man whom the other officers of the company wanted, but he failed to reach, getting 17 votes to Pratt's 23. Just what the outcome of the matter will be is not known. Pratt was selected at a previous election, but being ordered to Columbus for examination, failed to pass, and the office was declared vacant. Pratt claims he was not given a fair show at the previous examination or he would have passed. His election last night means that he will have to face the examiners again, and a merry time is looked for before the matter is settled.

At that time, it had only been thirty-three years since the end of the Civil War. Scioto County had contributed 2,216 of its sons to that cauldron—not all of them came back. We do not know what fathers told their sons of war, but one father whose son was in Company H wrote to Colonel Alonzo Coit, the commander of the Fourteenth Ohio National Guard Regiment (later redesignated the Fourth Ohio Volunteer Infantry Regiment after its mobilization for Federal service) and gave his opinion that his boy was not stout enough to physically withstand the rigors of a military campaign and should be exempted. The request was denied, but one can assume such sentiment was felt by other families for their sons. But perhaps the young men themselves felt that this coming war waged to free the Cuban people from bondage gave them the chance for adventure and to fight for a good cause, just like their fathers had in the Civil War. Like their fathers before them, glory would be theirs. Their fathers had freed the slaves, and they would free the Cubans. They would have stories to tell their children. Young men have that expectation.

The newspapers built up the cause for waging a campaign to free the oppressed Cuban people from their bondage to Spain. Long before the *Maine* exploded, the public was smothered with stories of Spanish outrage and revolutionary heroics. Headline ink aroused Americans. Referring in 1895 to a Spanish gunboat that shot at an American merchantman who was hauling a cargo of bananas and mustard seed, Joseph Pulitzer's *New York World* barked the

COLONEL A. B. COIT.

Colonel Alonzo B. Coit was the commander of the Fourth Ohio Volunteer Infantry, which Company H was attached to. *Taken from* The Story of the War of 1898, *by W. Nephew King, Lieutenant, U.S. Navy. New York: Peter Fenelon Collier & Son, 1900. This photograph and text album are owned by Michael Lewis, Boneyfiddle Military Museum, 421 Front Street, Portsmouth, Ohio, 45662.*

Contemporary publications inflamed the public's passions and romanticized the war. *From the Library of Congress.*

headline "Our Flag Fired On—The Nation Insulted." The *New York Sun* declared Spain needed "a sharp and stinging lesson at the hands of the United States." The *Chicago Tribune* called the shooting another outrage committed by "hot-blooded Spaniards." The *Milwaukee Sentinel* called the incident a "hostile and insolent act." The U.S. Congress debated the issue of an independent Cuba almost nonstop. Congressional resolutions poured out, decrying Spain and supporting Cuban revolution.

The clatter continued until 1898. When riots broke out in Havana in January, William Randolph Hearst of the *New York Journal* falsely stated the disturbances were aimed at the United States. Hearst and others, notably Theodore Roosevelt, the assistant secretary of the navy, openly called for war. Just prior to the sinking of the *Maine*, Hearst was alleged to have told his reporter in Cuba, Frederick Remington, "You furnish the picture, and I'll furnish the war."[6]

The administrations of both President Grover Cleveland and President William McKinley eschewed war with Spain, but by 1898, the nation's creep toward belligerency had turned into a downhill slalom. Relentless bellicosity followed by the *Maine* disaster and diplomatic blunders virtually ensured war. The country was up for it. Scioto County, Ohio, was up for it.

4

OFF TO WAR

Captain Robert Stanley Pritchard had his orders. He was to assemble his company at the armory at 8:00 a.m. on Tuesday, April 26, and they were to be ready to leave for Columbus at 10:28 a.m. on the Norfolk and Western Railroad. It was not the first time Company H had been called to arms. In early June 1894, the sheriffs of Guernsey and Belmont Counties appealed to Governor William McKinley for assistance in suppressing labor riots in a two-week deployment with other Ohio units that came to be known as the Wheeling Creek Campaign.[7] But this time was different. No one got hurt in that little labor scuffle. The Cuban conflict, however, was going to be a real war. They knew they were going to be sent far away, to a place that was strange to all of them. They knew some might not come back. There would be no more boring drills, marching this way and that, and Captain Pritchard would no longer have to send out patrols each meeting to scour the city for delinquent members.[8] At 8:00 a.m. on Sunday morning, Captain Pritchard called his men to attention. The entire company fell into formation. Their average age was twenty-three. The lowliest private was paid $13 a month, and their captain was paid $150 a month. Citizens soon began gathering around the armory.

Captain Pritchard had wisely begun preparing Company H and the citizens of Scioto County early for the departure of the soldiers. He signed up new recruits, quickly bringing the company up to the strength required by the army's guidelines at the time. When the call-up came and Company H began to assemble at its armory, Reverend Alderson of the Second

Presbyterian Church arrived and conducted Sunday services. A choir sang "Nearer My God to Thee." The congregation of the Second Presbyterian Church promised to send each member of the company a small copy of the New Testament. Even a few encouraging words from the local representative of the Internal Revenue Service was made. The spiritual impact this made on the soldiers can only be guessed. He promised to write a newsletter and send it each week, reporting the latest "goings on" back home. The inspirational part of the assembly ended at around noon with the hymn "Jesus, Lover of My Soul," a benediction and everyone joining in to sing "America." Sergeants Andrew Foster and Forest Briggs took command in the afternoon and put the company through a drill. They were dismissed at 5:00 p.m. and ordered to report back at 7:00 a.m. the next day.

A crowd started gathering early on Monday, and it only grew larger. Portsmouth took on a holiday-like atmosphere. Businesses and factories were short-staffed; some even shut down for the day. Schools were closed. A local band serenaded the crowd. Buildings, wagons and carriages were decked out in patriotic banners, bunting and flags. An occasional Cuban flag could be seen. Some local schoolboys marched down Chillicothe and Second Streets with a banner that read, "To Hell with Spain." Young girls handed out small flags for people to carry and pin on their lapels. The populace was swollen with patriotism. The throng was described as being just as passionate and fervent as an earlier generation had been for the sendoff of soldiers in 1861. Through all the festivity, the soldiers of Company H packed their mess kits, knapsacks and equipment and went through the paces of more drills, with breaks to eat and enjoy the band. They were dismissed early with orders to go home and take care of their affairs, but they were to stay close. The diary of Captain William Moore, a riverboat captain, noted that Private William M. Peebles stopped by his shop to say goodbye. The young Peebles had married into the family.

So, on Tuesday, April 26, 1898, a bright day, with fifteen strokes of the courthouse bell and a blast of the sirens of the Selby Shoe Factory and city waterworks, Company H formed up at the armory at the northwest corner of Fifth and Chillicothe Streets. With a new flag that was given to them by the local Women's Relief Corps and a bouquet of flowers for each soldier, the men took up their gear and shouldered their rifles. The order was given, and off they stepped. Marching with them were four bands, two drum corps, Union veterans of the Grand Army of the Republic (GAR), the Uniformed Knights of Pythias, former members of Company H and any number of young boys. They marched westward, down Fifth Street, turned

Company H, 4th OHVI : April 26, 1898
Marching east at Second and Court Sts,
Portsmouth, Ohio en route to the 10th St. train station
to embark for Columbus to
depart for the Spanish-American War

This is the iconic image of Company H marching off to war. Notice the rider holding aloft the Cuban flag. *This image came from a postcard that was purchased from Copies Galore, 709 Fourth Street, Portsmouth, Ohio.*

left on Market Street and then left on Second Street. A black-and-white photograph that was taken at the time shows crowds lining the sidewalks. A lone color bearer led the formation on horseback, holding aloft the Cuban flag. They then turned left on Chillicothe Street and marched up to Government Building Roadway to assemble on Government Square (now the Esplanade). A photograph of the formation on Government Square shows the front rank kneeling and the rear ranks standing. In front of the men stood a single individual, undoubtedly Captain Robert Stanley Pritchard. Perhaps he and his troops were listening to the prayers and stirring words of some of the local notables who were exhorting the boys to be brave, smite the foe and free the Cuban people from the yoke of wicked Spain.[9]

With the ceremony on Government Square over, the boys of Company H had a train to catch. Falling back into formation, they marched down Gallia Street, turned left on Waller Street and then moved up to Ninth Street making a left. After a few blocks they turned right onto Chillicothe Street, moving a block up to Tenth Street, and turning right, they went straight back to Waller Street, outlining the three sides of the perimeter of Tracy

Above: Company H assembled on Government Square (now the Esplanade) during its march to the train station. Notice their hats; these were later exchanged with floppy-brimmed "headgear" that was typically associated with the Spanish-American War. *Courtesy of the Southern Ohio Museum and Cultural Center, Portsmouth, Ohio.*

Opposite, top: Another view of Company H on Government Square. Captain Pritchard is probably the one standing in front of his troops. *Courtesy of the Southern Ohio Museum and Cultural Center, Portsmouth, Ohio.*

Opposite, bottom: The crowd dispersing from Government Square. One of the bands in the parade is in the lower right corner of the image. In the background are the church steeples of Bigelow United Methodist Church (*left*), currently renamed Grace Community Church at Bigelow, and the Evangelical United Church of Christ (*right*). Only the steeple of the Bigelow Church remains after a strong wind toppled the Church of Christ steeple on January 11, 2020. *Courtesy of the Southern Ohio Museum and Cultural Center, Portsmouth, Ohio.*

Park. A formation of the GAR saluted them as they passed. A few blocks later, they arrived at the train station at the northwest corner of Waller and Tenth Streets, where the N&W train sat, steamed up and already loaded with Company I, Seventeenth Ohio National Guard from Lancaster.[10] Family and friends crowded around them as they boarded. Copious tears,

Left: A quaint postcard image of a soldier saying farewell to his sweetheart. *The author found this postcard at Ghosts In The Attic, an antique shop at 518 Second Street, Portsmouth, Ohio.*

Below: This postcard was mailed to Cecil Smith at 1301 Kinney Street in Portsmouth, Ohio, from Garfield Baker. *The author found this postcard at Ghosts In The Attic, an antique shop at 518 Second Street, Portsmouth, Ohio.*

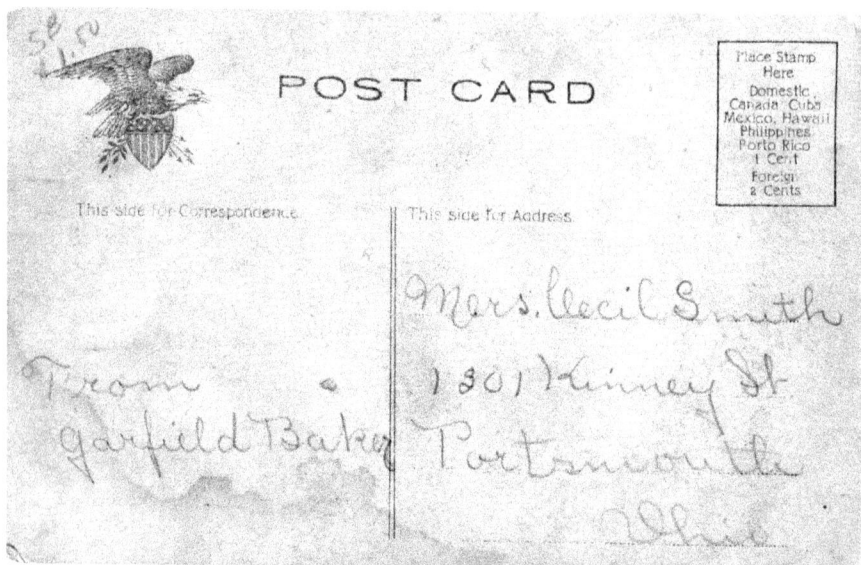

hugs and handshakes were all around. Baskets of food were passed up to the train's windows. With whistle and smoke, "with stout hearts and eager faces," Company H, "the boys," departed, leaving behind the waving white handkerchiefs of the people of Scioto County.

5

CAMPING OUT

Corporal Elbert Patterson's father was the editor of the *Portsmouth Daily Times*. Corporal Patterson's long letter about the train trip north was printed. A notable event of the trip came when the train stopped in Circleville to offload Company I and take on Company M, and during the company's journey to Columbus on the way to war, Lieutenant Pratt and Private Kelly lost their hats. Otherwise, the trip was described as "wearisome." Cheering crowds at various train depots slowed the train down. It finally arrived around 3:30 p.m. After detraining, the company was marched to an auditorium and given supper. The cook was Company H's own armorer Edward McGuire. The excellence of the meal was expounded on, but rations were short. Lieutenant Pratt dug into his pocket to augment the servings, earning the gratitude of every man of the company. They had to stay in the auditorium for the next two days while their campsite was being prepared. Corporal Patterson wrote that every member of Company H was in good shape and eager to go to the front. With the help of Privates Charles Wilheim and Reed M. Davidson, Patterson attempted to regularly furnish the *Times* with all that went on in camp. Floyd Thurman, a newspaperman for the *Portsmouth Blade*, had joined up with the company and also promised firsthand reports.

On April 23, 1898, President William McKinley asked Congress for a declaration of war against Spain. It came two days later. At the time, the army was proportionally smaller to the country's population of 73 million than it had been at the beginning of any other American war. The call went out to

The train with Company H stopped in Lucasville for a rousing send-off. *Courtesy of Jim Detty, David Huffman and Linda Jennings; Postcard History Series: Scioto County; and the Lucasville Area Historical Society, Lucasville, Ohio.*

the states for a volunteer force of 125,000. Among the states, Ohio sent the fourth-largest force. Company H and the Fourth Ohio Volunteer Infantry Regiment became part of a large buildup of Ohioans from all regions of the state. Around seven to eight thousand Buckeye soldiers settled into Bullitt Park, a five-hundred-acre site on the east side of Columbus in an area that is now known as Bexley. In honor of Governor Asa S. Bushnell, the encampment was named Camp Bushnell.

"The boys" of Company H settled into their assigned area and began the routine of a soldier's camp life. From April 26 to May 16, reveille came at 5:30 a.m., and taps came at 10:00 p.m. In between was breakfast, sick call, police duty (picking up trash that was lying around the campsite), guard duty, drill, lunch, in-school military instruction, more drill, cleaning stables and watering horses, formations, supper and a late afternoon parade after which there was free time. Daily rosy reports and gossip about the soldiers were sent back to the Portsmouth newspapers. "Company H is the noisiest of the regiment and had the fewest sent to the guardhouse." When Private

Asbury Davidson was on guard duty, he accidently bayoneted a member of Company B in the leg. This was the first trip that Adolph Reinert had ever taken without his dog. Edward McGuire wrote his lady friend on Ninth Street every day. Charles "Mugs" Maguire received six letters in one day, each from a different woman. Ralph Calvert wrote a letter to his dog. Company H beat Company B in a football game. A twenty-mile hike was cancelled due to cold and rainy weather. Captain Pritchard returned to Portsmouth to get more recruits to replace those who had failed the physical examination. "Hucksters" who came into camp trying to "skin" the soldiers ended up having their wares stolen. Five members of Company I were drummed out of camp after they said that the only reason they had joined up was to have a good time. The soldiers found a stray dog and adopted it as their mascot; they branded its side with "CO H." Someone took the cooking utensils of Company K (despised by all, it was said) and threw them in the water closet. Sergeant Andrew Foster, Corporal Charles Noel and Private J.W. Long were hauled before the Board of Inquiry to tell what they knew about the mysterious disappearance of Company K's mess chest, but they played dumb. Camp regulations were made stricter, and fewer men

A typical inspection of troops. The unit is unknown. *This image was taken from* The Story of the War of 1898, *by W. Nephew King, Lieutenant, U.S. Navy. New York: Peter Fenelon Collier & Son, 1900. This photograph and text album are owned by Michael Lewis, Boneyfiddle Military Museum, 421 Front Street, Portsmouth, Ohio, 45662.*

were seen outside the lines. The fishing wasn't good in Alum Creek. The camp hospital was filling up with soldiers who had measles and colds. The weather alternated from cold and rainy to hot. A couple of days of constant rain turned the camp into a swamp.

While Company H endured the alternating weather and the mischief that came with living among young men, the good citizens of Portsmouth and Scioto County had not forgotten their soldier boys. Relatives and friends streamed into camp, bringing fruit, pies, cakes, jellies and chicken. The local chapter of the Daughters of the American Revolution shipped boxes of cheese, candy, bonbons, butter, oranges, tobacco and cigars by express on the N&W railroad. A businessman even sent two bunches of bananas. So many people from all over Ohio were streaming into Camp Bushnell to visit their favorite sons that the railroad had to run an extra train. Some passengers had to stay overnight in Columbus because the railroad cars were overcrowded. On May 14, 1898, the *Daily Times* reported that at least a hundred visitors came by the Company H campsite every day.

The spiritual welfare of the soldiers was not neglected. The copies of the New Testament that had been promised by the Second Presbyterian Church had arrived. Back home, church sermons sent up prayers for the safe return of every soldier. Reverend J.D. Herron of All Saints Episcopal Church gave a mesmerizing sermon that came to be called "A Righteous War." An author with the initials B.S. published a poem titled "The Soldier's Farewell," with a supplication to God to keep the brave boys of Company H safe. Every Catholic church received a letter from its archbishop that was to be read out during Sunday services; it encouraged prayers for victory and the safe return of all soldiers.

Scioto County's patriotism induced more action than just the support of Company H. Even before war was declared, the sense that it was coming spurred the African American community of Portsmouth to start organizing its own company. They requested to be attached to the Ninth Ohio Volunteer Infantry Battalion (Colored). Portsmouth's Mayor Glidden encouraged the expansion of the National Volunteer Reserve.[11] Citizens from Otway, Mount Joy and Rarden turned in applications to join up. Emulating other cities across the country, Portsmouth set up a committee to put together a "Dewey Day," which celebrated the crushing victory of Admiral George Dewey over the Spanish fleet at Manilia Bay, Philippines.

Company H knew it was getting close to something important. Skirmish drills were added to its marching drills. On May 9, the company no longer belonged to the Ohio National Guard; it was officially mustered into the

Five "boys of Company H." *From left to right*: Private John Wesley Kinney, Corporal William P. Reed, Artificer Harry W. Donaldson, First Sergeant Russell C. Newman and Private Clifford M. Kinney. *Courtesy of the Portsmouth Public Library, Portsmouth, Ohio.*

military of the United States and became the Fourth Ohio Volunteer Regiment. As far as the federal government was concerned, the company was to be renamed Company E, but the familiar Company H was too ingrained in the minds of the soldiers and folks back home. The feds relented—Company H it would always be.

On May 13, the hustle and bustle of preparing to break camp started. In twenty minutes, personal belongings were packed. The regiment formed up on the drill field, and equipment was inspected. Inadequate and broken items were replaced with new ones. Each man was issued a half of a tent, so two were needed to pair up to make a two-man shelter. National guard uniforms were exchanged for federal tan trousers and blue flannel shirts. Yellow regular army blankets were issued. The soldiers had much anticipation about being paid. Finally, they hoped, they were going to have some money in their pockets. And there was more to eat.

As is common to those who have experienced military life, it turned out to be another "hurry up and wait." Three more days passed before the company left Camp Bushnell. Meanwhile, the cakes, jellies and rolls kept pouring in. Photographs of Company H members were taken. William D. McMonigle was made wagoner, and Harry W. Donaldson was made artificer.[12] Samuel A. Williams and Edward M. "Neddy" McGuire became buglers. Henry "Fatty" Morrison weighed 247 pounds. The company voted to present Lieutenant Pratt with a new sword as a token of their respect, as he had not hesitated to dig into his own pocket to buy supplies when they came up short. In a letter to the *Daily Times*, it was also deemed necessary to mention that a certain Miss Emma Nagelsen of Columbus was the frequent guest of Captain Pritchard. She often rode her bicycle to camp in the morning and didn't leave until evening.

6

SOUTHLAND

T he last major victory of the Confederate army after its defeat at Gettysburg occurred along the Chickamauga River in northwest Georgia. The only thing that kept the Rebel victory from being a complete rout of the Union army was the steadfastness of the "Rock of Chickamauga," General George Henry Thomas. When the United States Army began assembling its troops on the Chickamauga River in preparation of the Cuban Campaign it named the camp after Thomas. Camp Thomas became the new home of Company H.

May 15, 1898, was the real deal. The Fourth Ohio Volunteer Infantry Regiment packed up its gear and marched out of Camp Bushnell around 4:15 p.m.; the regiment then headed west down Broad Street and toward the train station that was five miles away. Stimulated by the unrestrained patriotism he saw, a newspaper reporter from the *Daily Times* (Portsmouth) headlined his report, "Stirred by the Wild Music of Fife and Drum." He said the passing of the soldiers was memorable.

> *It will live so long as time lasts....Mothers and sweethearts...their eyes filled with tears....Sons and lovers going away, perhaps never to return....* [It was] *the most remarkable demonstration ever witnessed in Columbus....As the train pulled out, cannon roared...the boisterous drums beat loud the marches of war...the heroic bugles sounded the wild music of battle....They were gone, and perhaps forever.*

The company arrived in Cincinnati around 7:00 p.m. Every little village along the B&O Rail Line, from Columbus to the Queen City, turned out to see the train cars full of soldiers pass by. At night, the men curled up in their yellow blankets and slept. When morning came, they were in Tennessee, 134 miles from Chattanooga. Letters to Portsmouth newspapers remarked on "the most beautiful scenery imaginable." Hills and mountains, waterfalls and rapids, little mountain streams, high rock cliffs, the Emery River, a light morning fog and the sunrise over the mountain summits. The more esthetically minded men of Company H were undoubtedly transfixed by the countryside they passed.

Lookout Mountain came into view as they approached Chattanooga. They entered the railyard, and they sat there for several hours. A band helped pass the time. Finally, around 2:00 p.m., they arrived at Camp Thomas, a few miles past the Georgia border. By the time everything was set up and supper was served, it was time for taps. It was hot. The next day, some of the men went swimming in the nearby creeks. All the heavy clothing that was suitable for Ohio weather was discarded. The men even got short haircuts. Fortunately for Company H, their "street" was shaded by large oaks and pines. For the first time, they would be sleeping on the ground.

The lax character of national guard life gave way to federalized army discipline. At Camp Bushnell, the men could occasionally miss drill and lie on their cots in their tents without serious reprimand. They also had the local YMCA providing various amusements, and as Captain Pritchard's lady visitor showed, Columbus was only a bicycle ride away. At Camp Thomas, anyone who missed roll call or drill would end up in the guardhouse. Corporal Clinton M. Searl ended up there just for making a face at Sergeant Briggs. Getting to the city charms of Chattanooga required a train ride; the city was ten miles away, and bicycles were scarce. The transition of the unit from the national guard to the United Sates Army brought seriousness to the business at hand, which was missing in Columbus. In Columbus, for the most part, they still felt at home, surrounded as they frequently were by family, friends and home-cooked meals that were delivered to their front tent flaps. Camp Thomas, situated as it was in the middle of a great Civil War battlefield, was more than just a great physical distance from home. It was a weighty step toward uncertainty.

A few Portsmouth locals had the wherewithal to make the journey to Georgia. At different times, attorney Theodore K. Funk; druggist Charles Seebohm; Captain A.B. Alger, the father of the Alger brothers; and J.L. Patterson, the editor of the *Portsmouth Daily Times*, visited. The druggist handed

A "street" scene of Company H at Camp Thomas, Chickamauga. *Courtesy of the L.M. Strayer Collection.*

out cigars. Two intrepid women, the mothers of Privates Emmett McKeown and Kinney Funk, located themselves close by and provided sewing services for the men during Company H's time in camp. Still, it wasn't home.

But wherever they are, soldiers are soldiers, and they'll do their best to skirt the rules, take the easy way out and find distraction wherever they can. Privates Frank Alger and Elbert Patterson waited until dark to sneak over to a lumber pile and steal some planks, which they put down on the bare ground in their tent. Soldiers from Company I discovered their crime, shoved them around and took the lumber. They had a two-mile empty-handed walk back to camp. Privates Arthur Welch and Charles Taylor corralled two wild pigs and brought them into camp to fatten them up.

Private Albert G. Herms was reported to have always had an interest in flowers. *Courtesy of the L.M. Strayer Collection.*

Many went hunting for relics from the Civil War. Private Emmett McKeown found a human arm bone. Wagoner McMonigle was put in charge of the four mules and two wagons the regiment had received to make the two-mile trip to the commissary and one-mile trip to the water spigot a lot easier. Private Albert Herms brought a large supply of flowers with him and wore a bunch every morning. Sergeant Russell C. Newman was made division quartermaster sergeant. Sergeant Walter H. Trimmer and Private Henry M. Morrison were the champions of horseshoes. Corporal Charles H. Reed and Private Adolph G. Reinert were the most successful Civil War relic finders. Captain Pritchard and Private Mathew W. Thompson hiked over to Snodgrass Hill and climbed an iron tower to look out over the battlefield. Some of "the boys" met Colonel Fred Grant, the son of General Ulysses S. Grant.[13]

From the day they arrived at Camp Bushnell (April 26) to the day they left Camp Thomas (July 22)—a total of eighty-eight days—Company H and the Fourth Ohio Volunteer Infantry Regiment waited to be called into action. They waited while great events passed them by. The navy destroyed the Spanish fleets in Manila Bay, Philippines, and outside Santiago, Cuba. The army landed in Cuba and fought battles at Las Guasimas, El Caney, Kettle Hill, San Juan Hill and Santiago. The Spanish army surrendered Santiago de Cuba to the United States. Fighting ceased in Cuba. Since they were well supplied with newspapers, the soldiers at Camp Bushnell and Camp Thomas could see their chance for glory lessening with each headline.[14]

"Victory at Manila," *New York Times*, May 2, 1898

"Landed at Last—The American Vanguard Safe on Cuban Soil," *Washington Times*, June 23, 1898

"The Spaniards are Fleeing from American Soldiers," *Philadelphia Inquirer*, June 25, 1898

"Battle of Santiago De Cuba Begins," *San Francisco Examiner*, July 1, 1898

"Occupation of Santiago a Matter of Hours Only," *Dayton Evening Herald*, July 2, 1898

"Cervera's Fleet Conquered at Last—Santiago Seems Doomed," *Baltimore Sun*, July 4, 1898

"It Is Settled! Terms Of Surrender," *Boston Sunday Globe*, July 17, 1898

It must have appeared to Company H that they had left behind family, friends and lovers for nothing. The way it was going, they would have no stories of heroics to pass on to their children and grandchildren, as their fathers had done after they defeated the Confederate army and saved the Union. So, they passed their time in drill, parades, inspections, mischief and in those staples of soldier life—complaining and spreading rumors.

The rumor that three of the water wells in camp had been poisoned proved false. A shortage of water kept the soldiers digging wells. Some water was piped in from a stream that was six miles away. By the time it reached camp, the pipes had been heated by the sun so much that the water was undrinkable but sufficient enough to wash cookware.

Wenonah Abbott was a female journalist who reported on the Spanish-American War. Rather than write in the gossip-like style of many other reporters, she addressed social issues. The *Daily Times* reprinted one of her columns that was mostly devoted to the trouble African American soldiers were having with southerners, but she also mentioned Company H. She said Company H was most welcome by southerners but that they should be careful of displaying their love of practical jokes, as southerners were more likely to shoot before seeing the point of any "matters of that kind."[15] Whatever puns and pranks that occupied the company's time at Camp Thomas, they apparently did not rise to the miscreant level of some other units. Company H was tasked with provost duty in Chattanooga, which required it to watch over those soldiers in the guardhouse who were given to fighting and insulting ladies on the streets of Chattanooga. On the company's way back to camp the next morning after one such guard duty, Privates Reed M. Davidson and Edward J. Reinhardt lingered too long in a strawberry patch and didn't made it back until suppertime.

Life in Camp Thomas mirrored the routine of the company at Camp Bushnell. They woke up to reveille and laid down to taps. Every morning, they stood in formation and listened to the band play the national anthem. The dirt street was raked. Blankets were thrown over poles to air out. Sick call came at 5:30 a.m., and mess call for breakfast came at 5:45 a.m. The first call for drill sounded at 6:20 a.m. Drills were done earlier in the morning and later in the afternoon due to the heat. The men went through their paces until 11:00 a.m. and then broke for lunch at 12:00 p.m. At 3:20 p.m., the bugle called the men to drill again. At 5:00 p.m., they broke, and fifteen minutes later they cleaned up the campgrounds. Part of the camp's routine was to burn straw bedding to kill pests and replace it with fresh bedding. Mess call came at 5:45 p.m., and at 6:30 p.m. the bugle sounded for dress parade. With bands playing and colors flying, the entire regiment paraded in front of the colonel. At 9:00 p.m., tattoo sounded, and at 9:30 p.m., the bugle sounded taps. Across the old battlefield, taps echoed from each regiment. No soldier could have possibly forgotten the haunting sound it must have made.

A YMCA tent had been erected that provided stamps, paper and amusements, such as checkers, puzzles and reading materials. Colonel Coit presented the regiment with a new stand of colors that was made of silk and adorned with the unit's streamers, each one naming the various call-ups of the regiment. These mobilizations were all about suppressing union labor strikes. It was donated by the Columbus Board of Trade. At the end of the presentation, three cheers were given for the donors and their "gallant" colonel. Private William H. Kelly, a mail carrier back in Portsmouth, was transferred to the post office department. His transfer came with a hefty pay raise. Private Distel, not being satisfied with his pay, took an extra job driving a beer wagon for Anheuser-Busch when he was off duty. Enough lumber was stolen from other units to make a table long enough for everyone in the company to eat at the same time. Corporal Joseph C. Bratt was in the hospital with a carbuncle on his neck. Some of the soldiers had to be revaccinated. Hygienic conditions in the camp began to decline, though it appeared that Company H maintained relatively good health.

After five weeks without a payday, the paymaster finally arrived. Wagons at the edge of camp that sold ice cream, lemonade, pies, cakes, strawberries and other good things were cleaned out. Some men took the train ride into Chattanooga so they could get a decent bath. Because

The Fourth Ohio Volunteer Infantry Post Office, Camp Thomas, Chickamauga. *Courtesy of the L.M. Strayer Collection.*

of the slow processing of paperwork, new recruits in the company did not get paid. Captain Pritchard borrowed money to give them. A certain Major Whittle from Chicago held Sunday services in the YMCA tent and urged the boys to be manly men and Christian soldiers. Some of the other regiments desecrated the Sabbath by playing baseball on Sunday. Company H helped break up a large dice game of Wisconsin soldiers and some civilians. Sergeant Russell Newman went back to Portsmouth to recruit more men after new army regulations mandated an increase in company strength to 106 officers and men. He was something of a celebrity in town, as he was the guest of honor at a reunion of Civil War veterans and feted with cigars and dinner at the Palace restaurant. New army regulations also mandated that any food sent to the soldiers from home was to be barred, as it was deemed unhealthy. Only army rations were to be served. Much grumbling ensued, followed by soldier conspiracies to skirt the rule, which they quickly did by sneaking off at night to get ice cream and soda water at Lytle, a small town within walking distance that had a post office and a couple of buildings. A mini mutiny of sorts broke out when the company made known that it would not drill unless it got provisions delivered on time. A delivery of potatoes and beans squelched the complaints.

Soon, it was the middle of June. Camp life became boring, and it was hot. Army doctors recommended that afternoon drill be suspended, but the officers ignored the advice. A heavy rain suppressed the heat for a while and gave the men the much-needed distraction of "frogging" in the swollen creeks—this was also a chance to supplement their army rations. Captain Pritchard obtained passes for the entire company to go into Chattanooga. They climbed Lookout Mountain and got caught in a violent thunderstorm. When they returned to camp, they had to sleep in the YMCA tent, as their bedding had been soaked by the storm. The tent flaps had not been closed. The Georgia rainy season had started, so it was hot *and* humid. The Portsmouth chapter of the Daughters of the American Revolution sent money to the company to be used only in the case that somebody became sick. Back in Portsmouth, Sergeant Newman accomplished his mission. He signed up thirty-seven new recruits, which met the new regulations for a full-strength infantry company of 106. He took them to Washington Court House, where they departed for Camp Thomas.

The first reported death in the regiment was that of one of the mules. At the funeral for the unfortunate beast, Company H was represented by Privates Albert M. Barber, Charles C. Taylor and Elton M. Bumgardner.

Full military honors were conferred, complete with taps. After the requirements of drill, various formations and camp duties were met, the men played baseball. Company H had a good team, beating teams from Wisconsin and Michigan. John F. Getz, who enlisted as a musician, was transferred to the Hospital Corps. Regimental bands played spirited tunes, such as "Marching Through Georgia" and "Onward Christian Soldiers." There was also a report that a private from an Illinois regiment was found to be a Spanish spy and was to be shot the following morning. Rumors about spies and the regiment leaving and going to Tampa, Florida; Charleston, South Carolina; Newport News, Virginia; the Philippines; Cuba; or Puerto Rico constantly swirled through Camp Thomas. False starts to get ready to break camp for "the front" came and went. Commands to pack gear, load wagons and mules with tents and all the stuff needed for a military campaign were given and then countermanded. Still, it was hard to miss that something was up. Waves of confusion seemed to be coming more frequently. The big push was coming. But where were they going to be pushed?

7

"Turmoil"

At first, even if Puerto Rico was mentioned at all in the newspapers, it was a short paragraph buried in the bigger story of Cuba. Major newspapers occupied themselves with the big picture. Stephen Crane, the author of *The Red Badge of Courage*, reported for the *New York World*. Richard Harding Davis, a celebrated war correspondent, sent dispatches to the *New York Sun*. Edward Marshall reported to William Randolph Hearst's newspaper, the *New York Journal*. When troops disembarked from Tampa, Florida, for the Cuban Campaign, there were eighty-nine newspapermen tagging along and nearly as many more followed.[16] With the battles in Cuba completed in less than a month, a lot of newspapermen were straining for reportable stories. Lucky for them, Puerto Rico lay just over the horizon.

Today, the campaign in Puerto Rico is largely forgotten. At the time, though, strategic planners saw the value in undertaking the conquest of the island. It denied the Spanish fleet the use of San Juan Harbor, and it isolated a reasonably strong Spanish garrison. Thinking further ahead, its excellent geographic location proved to be an excellent possession for the United States.

So it was that Company H played its part in the grand strategy of invading, conquering and occupying the island of Puerto Rico.[17] The soldiers in Company H gave little thought to grand strategy, but they noted with interest that 800,000 rounds of ammunition were received by the ordnance department and some were distributed to the First Ohio Calvary as it left for Tampa, Florida. The rest of the ammunition was to be used for target practice on a firing range that was being set up. Shooting matches were organized between the three companies in the battalion. Company H finished second. Corporal Byron D. Shriver and Private William L. Cole had the highest scores in the company. At some point during the shooting match, Private Harvey N. Will was "shot" by a skunk. Later, the men began conducting target practice from rifle pits.

On July 1, 1898, all of the newspaper reporters were escorted out of camp. The enlisted soldiers, such as Sergeant Wilhelm, Corporal Thurman and Private Patterson, who all had credentials that allowed them to send dispatches to their hometown newspapers, were ordered to cease these operations. Corporal Thurman, writing for the *Portsmouth Blade*, filed a dispatch with his paper, saying he had no intention of complying with this order. News about Company H still got through in the form letters that family members allowed the newspapers to print. The "blackout" order did not accomplish the desired suppression of news.

The rumor was passed around the company for about two weeks, and then it came true. It became the sensation of the camp. On June 21, Captain Pritchard and Lieutenant Pratt tendered their resignations. The reason—"business matters." That lame excuse gave way to "the old trouble," suggesting something was bubbling beneath the surface. Whatever the reason or reasons, it was highly unlikely to be for any significant disaffection among the ranks. Both officers seemed to have been highly regarded by their men. Prior to Pratt's departure, the enlisted men presented him with a sword they had voted to give him when they were in Camp Bushnell. Captain Pritchard was always described in positive terms by the enlisted men. When he got off the train in Portsmouth, he was serenaded by the River City Band, presented with a sword by a group of citizens who esteemed his service and escorted to his home.

The War Department had allowed Captain Pritchard to withdraw his resignation, but Colonel Coit relieved him of command anyway, citing the captain's refusal to obey orders. His alleged disobedience may have stemmed from the failure of the enlisted men in the mess tent to boil water before washing pots and pans, an order that the colonel had directed the captain to see was carried out. This singular transgression seemed to have been more of a final straw in friction between Captain Pritchard and Colonel Coit. The enlisted men wrote home about it. The captain gave the order to the mess detail to boil water, but they failed to convey the order to the soldiers who were relieving them; hence, when the colonel passed by the mess tent and saw that the water was not being boiled, he concluded that

Captain Pritchard was derelict in his duty. A short inquiry by the colonel would have revealed the matter to have been nothing more than a failure in communication between enlisted men rather than Captain Pritchard's neglect. Should he have been reprimanded for not following up on his order to the first mess detail? Most likely, yes. But to relieve him from command over water that was not boiled after there had never before been any indication that he was derelict of orders seemed severe. Perhaps there was more to the story.

Theodore K. Funk was a high-profile attorney in Portsmouth and was well connected. He counted among his friends Governor Bushnell. Attorney Funk had no hesitation in advocating for his cause—whatever the case. He was also the father of Kinney P. Funk, who enlisted in Company H as a private.[18] The telegram from the governor's office that announced the promotions of those who eventually replaced Captain Pritchard and Lieutenant Pratt was sent to attorney Funk. He had to have been pleased to see that his son had been promoted from private to second lieutenant. The jump of Kinney P. Funk from lowly private to officer seemed to surprise some. More attuned readers of newspaper commentaries and letters from soldiers must have sensed discord and low morale within Company H and the advocacy of Funk's father for his son. An editorial in the July 16 edition of the *Daily Times* was quite blunt: "When the facts causing the turmoil that has discouraged and disheartened the brave boys of Company H are fully known, the people of this city and county will rise up in denunciation of the politicians who set to work the day the boys left this city to relegate Stanley Pritchard to private life and send him home in disgrace."

When Private Funk was presented his commission by Colonel Coit, promoting him to second lieutenant, it was done in front of the entire regiment and with words that let everyone know that the promotion was political, unjustified and would cripple the unit. Such words from the commanding officer in front of the entire unit could only have humiliated the new second lieutenant and created lasting animosity.

The informal and gossipy style of the reporter/soldiers in the company who sent dispatches back to their newspapers did not usually mention "turmoil." The dispatches were overwhelmingly lighthearted. A company member needed a bath. Another always cracked jokes. Yet another had a big appetite—and so on. It seemed that every member of Company H had their name mentioned in some amusing, mischievous way in the newspapers—all except Kinney P. Funk. When perusing the newspapers, one can only find a few straightforward references to

Private/Lieutenant Funk. Such mentions included that his father visited him at Camp Thomas when he was sick, he was on orderly duty one day, he was promoted from private to second lieutenant and, after commissioning, he was presented a sword by "his many friends," who were unnamed by the *Daily Times*. Then, two weeks later, General P. C. Hains, the commanding general of all volunteers, and Colonel Coit requested Lieutenant Funk's resignation, the colonel citing his inability to physically perform his duties.[19] He resigned soon after arriving in Puerto Rico and got on a ship that was heading north.[20] Conjecture suggests that from the beginning, Private Funk's father, Theodore Funk, was dissatisfied that his boy was a mere private and began a personal campaign to elevate his rank to officer—even to the point of getting the governor to decree the promotion. The results of the "turmoil" could not have pleased his father.

As for Lieutenant Pratt, not long after returning to Portsmouth, he enlisted in the Fourth Kentucky Volunteer Infantry and became the drum major of the regimental band. The *Daily Times*, on July 7, noted that in between Camp Thomas and Portsmouth, Pratt had stopped by Governor Bushnell's office and given him the "facts"—whatever they may have been. We can suppose that Captain Pritchard returned to his bicycle shop at 222 Chillicothe Street (now the location of the Hurth Apartments). Among the dignitaries who met him as he got off the train from Camp Thomas was Theodore Funk.

So it came to be that Company H departed Camp Thomas without the captain who had been its commander long before the declaration of war with Spain and its second in command who had been elected to that position by a majority of the enlisted men earlier in the year. The man who came in second in that election, Second Lieutenant James A. Smith, was their new leader. He was promoted to captain on July 26. The company went through the remainder of its service with one officer. Colonel Coit had recommended Private Reed and Sergeant Newman for commissions to replace Pritchard and Funk. The unwillingness of the commissioning powers to grant the colonel's recommendations could have been due to anything, from a lack of confidence in the colonel's judgment to a vindictive desire to diminish his stature in the eyes of his command after his rebuke of Private Funk's qualifications for an officer's commission in front of the regiment. With some in Company H, there appears to have been lasting bitterness over the "turmoil" at Camp Thomas. After the war and the return of the company, the *Daily Times* reported a threat of physical violence against Colonel Coit if he followed through with a planned visit to Portsmouth to attend the Company H Military Ball. He went anyway—and without incident.

8

MOVING OUT

F inally, Company H was leaving Camp Thomas. The hard labor that came with breaking camp—only to reverse the process time and again—mercifully ended. The company's destination was Puerto Rico via Newport News, Virginia. On the morning of July 22, after nearly ten weeks of drilling in oppressive heat, boring repetitive routine and enduring the camp's "turmoil," Company H marched out of Camp Thomas, down a dust-choking road, to the train station. There, the men waited. The next day, the men boarded Pullman cars and headed to war. There were three trains—one for each battalion. Being in the Second Battalion, Company H boarded the second train. With bunks to sleep in instead of the hard ground and straw in tents, the men of the company felt that they were in luxury.

Again, as it had on the company's journey to Camp Thomas, the beauty of the countryside rolling by impressed the men. They could lower the windows and feel the wind and wave at people and cows they passed. They shouted out, "On to Puerto Rico!" All the way to their Virginia port of departure, the reporter/soldiers and individual letters home mentioned the splendor of the land they passed through. Kentucky bluegrass and the grandeur of the New River and Allegheny Mountains were all specifically mentioned. Also reported was how happy the men were to be on their way. There must have been a great sense of liberation from hot Camp Thomas. Again, folks in towns and villages along the way came out to wave them on to their destiny. Homes and buildings were decorated with patriotic bunting and flags. There were so many food baskets handed up to them everywhere the train stopped that the three days of army rations that had been issued to them before leaving Camp Thomas were thrown away. They gave their names and addresses to pretty girls. It was common for young girls to crowd up to the cars and trade roses, hair ribbons, fans and handkerchiefs for souvenirs such as brass buttons and hard tack biscuits. At Farmers, Kentucky, a man gave Sergeant Forest C. Briggs a package containing a stick of dynamite, and he was told to use it to blow the Spaniards to hell. Sergeant Walter H. Trimmer grabbed the dynamite and threw it in a creek.

The company rolled into Lexington, Kentucky, changed over to the Chesapeake and Ohio Railroad and headed to Ashland, Kentucky. In plenty of time, the word had gotten out to Portsmouth that "the boys" were headed their way. A few made it to Lexington to cheer them on, but it was in Ashland that the action really got wild. An estimated four hundred people showed up to greet the train that was hauling their favorite sons to war. Every room in town was taken. The train was late. Some waited and partied through the night with the help of a nickel-in-the-slot music box. Some had to go back to Portsmouth to be at work the next day. When the train finally arrived around 5:30 p.m. the next day, the crush was on to get up to the train cars and convey baskets full of food and items. But it was the first train carrying the First Battalion that pulled in. A so-called humorous incident occurred when some folks, who were unaware that their soldiers were not on that train, passed up their baskets to First Battalion soldiers, who generously promised to convey them to the intended recipients—which, of course, did not happen. This went on for a while until some of the officers discovered the scam and put a halt to it. It is a fair guess that the incident was not very humorous to the donors and the expected Company H beneficiaries. Sometime around 8:30 p.m., the second train bearing the Portsmouth soldiers arrived. It was pure revelry. Soldiers poured from the train doors and jumped out of windows to mingle with the crowd and look for loved ones who were looking for them. They had thirty minutes to hold and kiss each other. One told of home without the other, and the other told of a soldier's life. The lemonade of Portsmouth was described as "splendid." Private Ralph W. Calvert managed to give a bird dog he had with him to his brother to care for until he returned. John Schmitt was so overwhelmed with patriotic fever that he immediately quit his job at the *Daily Times* and submitted his application to join. Later, he reported his success at becoming a soldier in Company H with the rank of private. Dusk was starting to close in, so a huge Wells light was set up to illuminate the scene. In no time, the bugler blew. Amid hurried farewells, hugs and kisses, "the boys" of Company H piled back into their Pullmans. They departed Ashland around 9:00 p.m. It had to have been a departure as certainly as emotional as the day they left Portsmouth. Indeed, it was perhaps more so. Who knew when—or if—they would see each other again?

Finally, the company was on its way. When crossing the mountains of West Virginia, the men ate the food that was given to them in Ashland. Private Asbury W. Davidson wrote a poem about it:

> *The boys are willing, dead willing*
> *To go to Porto Rica and die.*
> *If they could only live long enough*
> *To eat another piece of mother's pie.*

They retired to their bunks. It must have been a slow train ride up the steep grades of West Virginia. Locomotives of that day lacked the power of subsequent machines, and stopping for repairs was common. When the men woke up, they were only still in West Virginia, climbing the mountains toward Clifton Gorge, Virginia. Once there, they were supplied with coffee and sandwiches. From there, it was all "downhill" on the way to Newport News. As they neared Charlottesville, Virginia, the men passed a woman waving a Confederate flag.

They arrived at Newport News on July 24 and pitched their tents at Camp Hains, about two hundred yards from the bay of the James River.[21] In an unsigned letter, a Company H soldier described the town as small but "tough" because of all the sailors who passed through there. For the Scioto County soldiers, it was a new, wonderful world near the ocean. The sights impressed the eyes of Private Barry J. Alger so agreeably that he said he could live the rest of his life near the coast. Back home, the best they could do for water was a big river that flooded them out of their homes every year. The men set up camp as fast they could and then rushed to the bay for a saltwater bath. It was not unusual to see two thousand soldiers at a time—either naked or in their underwear—taking a bath in the James River Bay. They wore their shoes to keep from being pinched by crabs and stepping on sharp oyster shells, and they watched out for stinging jelly fish. They gazed at the cruiser USS *Minneapolis* lying offshore. Roll call found many soldiers missing from formations. They scattered about the town and shore taking in the sights. They could gaze out over the bay, where thirty-six years ago, the Civil War ironclads *Monitor* and *Merrimack* bounced cannonballs off each other. Their steel offspring lay anchored in the bay. They were invited aboard some of them. They marveled at the large dry docks of the Newport News shipping industry. Discipline was light. Apparently,

Private Louis Distel was still with them. Back at Camp Thomas, he had been sentenced to seven months imprisonment for sleeping on guard duty. There is no mention anywhere of whether or not he served the sentence. In a letter to his parents, Private Bumgardner reported seeing a six-foot-long shark and a two-foot-long artillery shell that had gone through the Battle of Santiago. The men received a sobering sight when wounded soldiers from the Battle of Santiago—some without arms or legs—passed by. Bumgardner and some fellow soldiers boarded a yacht and went out into the bay. There they saw a "submarine" boat. The bay was starting to fill up with warships and transports. Bumgardner learned that Company H would be transported to Puerto Rico on the transport ship USS *St. Paul*. Commanding the men would be Captain Charles Sigsbee, the captain of the ill-fated USS *Maine*.

Aside from the novelty and diversions of coastal life, soldier life was still soldier life. Some things were inescapable. As at Camp Thomas in Tennessee, the parade grounds at Camp Hains in Virginia were miserably hot. There were no shady trees on the tent-lined street—just hot sand. Drilling, marching, formation, "fatigue" duty, digging "sinks" (latrines and trash receptacles) and loading and unloading supplies were nonetheless indispensable to the army, if not to the soldier. At Camp Hains though, one big thing was different. The men knew that they were going to board that big ship out in the bay, and as Corporal Thurman put it in a letter to the *Portsmouth Blade*, they were going to sail from the "Sweet Land of Liberty." Thurman reported that all of his Company H comrades were in good health and anxious to get to "the front." He also reported that it might not have been so healthy for Company M (from Circleville, Ohio). When only twenty-six members of Company M showed up for parade, it was suspected that yellow fever or smallpox had struck camp. Thurman's dispatch home seemed to be the first of all the Company H letters and reports to ominously mention serious disease. It might have dampened the anxiety of the folks back home if he had added that perhaps the Company M boys were just loafing on the beach.

Not with Company H were three of their friends, as they had been transferred to the Hospital and Ambulance Corps. Adolph G. Reinert, Henry H. Winters and Harry W. Donaldson traveled apart from the rest of the company. They went through Charleston, West Virginia, to Newport News, Virginia, and boarded the USS *Massachusetts*, a ship that had recently transported P.T. Barnum's circus animals and was then crowded with mules and horses. Their voyage to Puerto Rico was miserable. The ship's captain got drunk and ran aground in Ponce, Puerto Rico. For the greater part of their time on the island, they worked in the hospital at Ponce, Puerto Rico.

VOYAGE TO WAR

T he time had come. Three days of seaside living had come to an end—too soon for those who may have seen themselves settling down by the bay after their wartime duties. The tent cities of Camp Bushnell and Camp Thomas were miles behind; perhaps in the mind of each Company H soldier, they were dream-like memories. There would be no more baskets of food held up to train windows, no more pretty girls waving flags, no more visitors from home. But as it does for all wartime volunteers, melancholy existed alongside an eagerness for battle. The men had cheerfully signed up for the unknown. They wanted to get to "the front." Back in Columbus, those who had been rejected for service for physical reasons were overwhelmingly unhappy. One such rejected man named Power Brown went so far as to follow the unit to Camp Thomas, where he worked in the mess tent and did everything he could to live the life of a soldier. He was well liked by everyone, despite the fact, it was said, that he never learned how to properly peel potatoes. It appears that he did not make it to Camp Hains.

The men struck camp, loaded their gear on wagons and marched a few miles to Point Comfort at the end of a sliver of land that was jutting out into the bay. They fully expected then and there to board and sail away— not so. In some army manual somewhere, there must be a regulation that says soldiers expecting immediate trouble-free movement must be taught the hard lesson of waiting. Some laid down on the sand to sleep, others took to the hard floor of a casino, all waiting for the dawn.

The next day, around 2:00 p.m., the bugle blew for assembly. In a column of four, the men marched down to the wharf, loaded into small transports called lighters and went out to climb aboard the *St. Paul*. It took almost an hour to get alongside. Once on board, they found themselves assigned to sleeping quarters four decks below in sweltering air that could not be tolerated for more than fifteen minutes. They stored their gear and spent most of the cruise topside amid a cool sea breeze all the way to Puerto Rico. They helped load a large supply of provisions and gear, including crates of Krag-Jorgensen rifles and ammunition.[22] Around 6:00 a.m. the next day, the *St. Paul* weighed anchor and began pulling out to open water.[23] Coming from farms, small villages and Portsmouth in Scioto County, we can infer that very few of them, if any, had ever been on a ship at sea. With the beat of the ship's engines beneath their feet, they lined up at the side rails to watch land and houses recede from the horizon; 1,425 miles ahead lay Puerto Rico. Who would return? Who would not?

The men were at sea for a week. With 381 sailors and nearly 1,300 soldiers on board a ship that was 553 feet, 2 inches long and 63 feet wide, living space was crowded. A month earlier, the *St. Paul* had taken the Eighth Ohio Volunteer Infantry (OVI) to Cuba. One of the sailors had befriended a soldier in the Eighth OVI and kept in touch with him. In a letter to his friend, he stated that the Fourth OVI, which included Company H, was not "the life and sociability the 8th was."[24] Apparently, to some of the sailors of the USS *St. Paul*, the Fourth OVI was boring.

In a letter home, Private Matthew W. Thompson described the voyage as smooth, with only a few suffering seasickness. Perhaps he was wanting to gloss over the reality of the voyage to his folks. For country boys and city boys who had never been to sea, the description by Sergeant Major Charles E. Creager is probably more accurate. Many, he said, could be seen "delivering all his stomach…into the deep blue sea."

There was gracious camaraderie between the sailors and soldiers. No one wanted to go below because of the oppressive heat. They slept and ate on the open deck. They learned the operations of their new Krag-Jorgensen rifles. There were plenty of provisions, but the menu was the same boring fare: canned baked beans, canned tomatoes, canned corned beef, hardtack and "poor" coffee. And it was bad. Much of it had spoiled after sitting in warehouses and then in the sun for extended periods of time. It was even "sickening" to look at. "Who," asked Sergerant Major Creager, "was responsible for this unnecessary suffering?" After the ship's bakers offered to sell bread to the soldiers, they took it on themselves to steal it. Many a peach pie came up missing. Not only were soldiers anxious to get ashore to join the fight, they were certain they would have something better to eat. The cheerful rumor was that one penny would buy seven bananas or two lemons. Though there was plenty of water on board, there was no ice.

In the early morning of August 1, after looking at nothing but featureless seascape for the past five days, the cry of land within sight went up. Soldiers rushed to the rails to see a small island off the Dominican Republic. Eastward, a few hours later, the harbor of Guanico, Puerto Rico, came into view. Finally, enemy territory was before them. From the harbor, a vessel could be seen headed toward the *St. Paul*. Could it have been a Spanish ship coming to engage them in their first battle of the war? Would this be their baptism of fire? The anticipation of early combat died away when it was identified as USS *Terror*, a rebuild monitor from the Civil War. A message was delivered that the *St. Paul* should continue to Ponce, the largest city on the island that was situated in the center of the island's southern coast. Mail was transferred to the *St. Paul* and off it went to what was anticipated to be the battle for Ponce. An hour later, they spied the USS *St. Louis* lying in the harbor of Ponce, and they learned that the city had surrendered without a fight. The fighting blood of Company H and the rest of the Fourth OVI cooled again. They spent the night on board the ship helping unload rifles. As it had back at Camp Thomas, it probably seemed that, with no apparent enemy to fight, great events were passing them by. Perhaps the next day would bring them their war.

With new orders, the *St. Paul* sailed forty miles east to the small port of Arroyo; it arrived there on August 3 and found several ships anchored, including the battleship USS *Cincinnati*. Rifles, ammunition, bayonets and belts that could hold one hundred rounds were issued. Lighters were brought alongside to transport soldiers ashore. This was it—finally. The invasion was on. The Fourth OVI was about to set foot on enemy soil. Once ashore, the plan was for the regiment's companies to advance about six miles inland the next day and battle the Spanish for the town of Guayama, a city of about five thousand. All, that is, except for Companies H and M. They unloaded the ship and loaded Studebaker wagons that were to be escorted to the rest of the regiment in Guayama. Company H became stevedores.[25]

The only officer in charge of Company H was Lieutenant Smith. New officers had not been appointed following the disruption of command back at Camp Thomas. All command decisions and orders from above fell on

THE PLAZA AND CATHEDRAL AT GUAYAMA. FROM THIS SQUARE GENERAL BROOKE'S FORCE ADVANCED AS SKIRMISHERS AND DROVE THE ENEMY TO THE HILLS BEHIND THE TOWN.

The plaza and cathedral in the center of Guayama, Puerto Rico. The Fourth Ohio Volunteer Infantry and Company H bivouacked in this area for almost two months. *This image was taken from* The Story of the War of 1898, *by W. Nephew King, Lieutenant, U.S. Navy. New York: Peter Fenelon Collier & Son, 1900. This photograph and text album are owned by Michael Lewis, Boneyfiddle Military Museum, 421 Front Street, Portsmouth, Ohio, 45662.*

him. It would not be surprising to find that he felt his responsibility was a heavy weight. There was some supposition in the dispatches back to local newspapers that the lack of command structure and the antagonisms in the company while at Camp Thomas caused a lack of faith in the company's usefulness in the Puerto Rican Campaign. For whatever reason, all of Company H, except for brothers and privates Barry J. and Frank K. Alger and Sergeant George McDonald, was left behind to help unload the *St. Paul* and load and guard the wagons. As they had been appointed color bearers for the regiment, the Alger boys and the sergeant were in on the initial advance against the Spanish soldiers, and they subsequently had the honor of hoisting the Stars and Stripes over the Guayama city building. Frank Alger wrote home about his, his brother's and the sergeant's introduction to war.

The regiment first came under fire from a Spanish ambush as they advanced on Guayama. It was "hot" for about an hour and a half. The bullets "whizzed around like bees." The regiment pushed aside the ambush and advanced on the town. The heat of the day caused many of the soldiers to discard equipment. Several collapsed from heat exhaustion. They swept through the town, driving back the Spanish, who kept a steady rate of fire as they pulled back. The Alger brothers and their sergeant took shelter in the mayor's office of the city hall, then climbed up on the roof and ran up the American flag. A reporter from *Harper's Weekly* took their photograph. Momentarily, the shooting had stopped while the brothers sat on the wall, watching the people below celebrate their freedom from Spain. Their ringside seat did not last long though, as the flag they raised also raised the ire of the Spanish soldiers, who started peppering the city hall. The men dove for cover amid bullets that hit so close, they flinched. An odd artillery weapon called a dynamite gun lobbed a few shells in the direction of the firing, which then ceased. The reaction of the townspeople was jubilation. "They yelled, they cried, the[y] laughed, hugged and kissed each other and yelled themselves hoarse with their cries of Viva America."[26] The townspeople gave the soldiers wine, brandy, bread, fish, cigars and cigarettes. The chief of police of the town was not so friendly. He shot a hole in the American flag that was flying atop the city hall and was promptly jailed in his own jailhouse. Soldiers helped themselves to "souvenirs" from the homes of unfriendly Spaniards. American casualties from the Battle of Guayama were five wounded, none killed. Everyone agreed that the enemy marksmanship was very bad. At that point, no member of Company H had been wounded or killed in battle. Nonetheless, death found another way.

A funeral procession on a Guayama street for an American soldier. Private Daniel H. Dodge was one of the several soldiers who were buried in a Guayama cemetery. *This image was taken from* The Story of the War of 1898, *by W. Nephew King, Lieutenant, U.S. Navy. New York: Peter Fenelon Collier & Son, 1900. This photograph and text album are owned by Michael Lewis, Boneyfiddle Military Museum, 421 Front Street, Portsmouth, Ohio, 45662.*

Daniel H. Dodge, a blue-eyed young man with red hair, was a private in Company H and a shoe cutter in civilian life. He lived in Portsmouth at 261 East Sixth Street. He answered the call for volunteers at the very beginning of the war. In a short letter home—his last—that was mailed to his brother, who was an attorney, he stated that he had been ill with seasickness ever since leaving Newport News. It may have been the beginning of typhoid fever, a serious disease that begins with contaminated food and water. Perhaps young Daniel contracted the typhoid germ as they were departing Camp Thomas, which had become fetid from the thousands of soldiers camped there. Or maybe he had eaten a tainted can of corned beef aboard the *St. Paul*. His sickly condition was obvious enough that when the ship pulled into the Arroyo Harbor, he was taken immediately ashore to a hospital. A week later, he died. His death created another controversy for Company H. The reporter for the *Portsmouth Daily Times*, Corporal Elbert Patterson, issued a dispatch to his newspaper, accusing the hospital staff of negligence. He also accused the regimental chaplain of enjoying a cigar in a drugstore when he should have been presiding over Dodge's funeral. The act of an enlisted man publicly criticizing those in rank above him—particularly those in senior rank—is not taken lightly by the army. Patterson was reduced to private, and court-martial proceedings were begun. The charge was for circulating a falsehood in regard to his superior officers. A flurry of letters from officers went out to the Dodge family, assuring them that everything medically and spiritually possible had been done for young Daniel. Trouble had found Company H again. First, there was the upheaval of command back at Camp Thomas. Then, there was the death of Dodge. This time, a lowly enlisted man had stirred the pot. Dodge was laid to rest in a wooden coffin in a designated lot that began to fill with other dead soldiers.

10

MOVING INLAND

P uerto Rico, "the most beautiful of the Greater Antilles," is a virtually
rectangular island that is about 108 miles long and 45 miles wide.
At the time of the conflict with Spain, the island's population was
about 900,000. Its three major cities were Ponce, the largest, in the middle
of the Southern coast; Mayaguez in the middle of the west coast; and San
Juan on the northern coast, a bit to the east of center. In the *Century*, the
largest circulated periodical of the time, the naturalist Frederick A. Ober
described the island as having "scene[s] of grandeur, tempered with the
melting loveliness of a tropical landscape...exuberant and diversified
vegetation...hot and humid...insects of questionable character."[27] There
were two seasons of the year, he said: "rainy and dry." As to the character
of the people, he quoted an unnamed author, describing them as "affable,
generous, hospitable to a fault," and another unnamed author said that the
climate induced the people toward laziness. He concluded his article with
the hope that the "all-conquering American" treats the Puerto Rican people
with respect. In the text that accompanies the photographs and drawings
compiled in *Leslie's Official History of the Spanish-American War*, the island's men
are described as indolent and the women as industrious.

Corporal Searl's articulate letters home said that the scenery, language
and people were so different from home that it felt like being in Puerto
Rico was "like...in a dream." It was the land of delicious coconuts,
bananas, pineapples, limes and fruits he never knew existed. Cows and
goats supplied the milk. Houses of brick were plastered on the outside

and often decorated with artistic curios and figures. The climate was "delightful," the soil was rich, the labor was cheap and the real estate was inexpensive. A person could make a lot of money in the sugar business. He was tempted, he said, to stay and invest his money—to grow along with the country. At least, he said, he would like to spend his winters there. Having taken Latin in school, he could somewhat understand the language. His curiosity was eclectic. He described the strangeness of starfish and sea urchins. He watched the natives grind their corn on flat rocks. Although they were behind the times in many ways, he noted that some of the finest oil paintings he had ever seen were there. Whether they were locally produced or brought over from Spain, he could not tell. Nevertheless, the prices for them were steep. He enjoyed eating sticks of raw sugar cane; it was the sweetest and juiciest thing he had ever tasted. Mothers gave their babies sticks of sugar cane to quiet them.

Another Company H soldier, Private Francis M. Bush, likewise found the soil fertile, and he saw a great potential for growth in the country, especially in the sugar industry. They made good wine, he said, but the rum was bad. Other soldiers were not so kind in their opinions. Private Isaac "Dusty" Krick said the people talked like "durned fools" because he could not understand them; he said if he ever got back to Portsmouth, he would never leave. Private Harry E. Adams was sick and tired of fruit and described the Spaniards as "sneaky." Another soldier, who signed his name as "Vint," called the locals "savages."[28]

The grand strategy for subduing Puerto Rico involved 18,000 American soldiers challenging approximately 8,000 Spanish soldiers and 9,000 poorly trained and unreliable Puerto Rican volunteers. When all was said and done, it took about 9,000 Americans to subjugate the Spaniards. Landings of troops occurred on the southern coast at Guanica, Ponce and Arroyo, the latter was where we found "the boys" of Company H, 105 strong.

The wagons, probably manufactured by Studebaker, with springs for the seat but not the wagon bed, were loaded and hitched to oxen. This was a laborious job, as the *St. Paul* was anchored five miles offshore. Company H had completed its first mission in the war against Spain. The company's next assignment required the men to safely deliver the wagons to the Fourth OVI, which was stationed in Guyama. It was a six-mile trek. The wagons bounced and rocked, and the oxen, strong beasts that they were, moved excruciatingly slow. Along the road to Guayama, the men gathered up discarded equipment. They arrived around midnight and slept under the wagons.

Company H settled in with its regimental comrades at Guayama. From the camp, the men sortied forth to scout for the enemy and forage for food. Sergeant Samuel A. Williams took out small scouting parties. On one such sortie, he did not find any Spaniards, but his patrol rounded up a sheep, a lamb, four chickens and a goat. He bragged that he and his comrades, Sergeant Foster, Corporal Searl and Privates Reed, Thurman and Mathews, brought in more meat than any other foraging party. Like every army before them, they supplemented their rations by "living off the land," which was another way of saying they either bartered, purchased or stole from the indigenous people. They also supplemented their rations through a market in Guayama, which afforded them fish, cheese, eggs, milk and yams.

Many women in the city had a brisk trade in providing laundry services; although, to the annoyance of the soldiers, after ironing they had a practice of piling the clothing into one large mixed-up pile. Many ended up with ill-fitting uniforms. Funds were scarce for some soldiers, so they washed their clothes and took baths in one of the three rivers there. Some citizens of the city opened up their homes to the soldiers for bathing amenities.

American and Spanish outposts were within rifle range of each other. Pot shots from the Spanish side were a nuisance—as, no doubt, were those from the Americans. The "enemy" that was wandering in between the lines at night normally ended up being a dead horse, cow or goat in the morning, all of which had a way of ending up in a stew. No American was killed or wounded in these nighttime battles.

Heavy rains that lasted for hours pounded the camp. And then, it quickly became very hot. Soldiers who were on sentry duty during the day wore out easily. Water came from springs in the surrounding mountains, but just like it had back at Camp Thomas, by the time the water reached them, it was hot. Scorpions and insects bedeviled the soldiers. The perils of camp life were more than just uncomfortable weather and tiresome inconveniences. One dark night, a soldier from Company D (from Marysville, Ohio) who was on sentry duty killed a soldier who failed to answer a challenge to identify himself. Sickness was also becoming an issue. Private Arthur R. Welch was in a Puerto Rican hospital, and Privates Fred M. Armstrong and David J. Johnson were sent to a hospital back in the United States. Sergeant Williams's letter home declared the hospital full with malaria and typhoid fever victims. Only one officer was left after the resignations of Pritchard and Funk, so First Lieutenant Charles O. Updyke of Company E (from Washington Court House, Ohio) was temporarily transferred to Company

H to assist Lieutenant Smith with command of the company until he got the hang of it and his official commission as captain came through. Lieutenant Updyke turned out to be very popular with the men; they were sorry to see him return to his own company.

The encampment around Guayama grew large. Aside from the infantry, the military hospital, cavalry and artillery, with all their horses and mules, arrived. Preparations began for a push on San Juan, which everyone was eager to do. News reached the regiment that Spain had sued for peace. In a dispatch to the *Portsmouth Blade*, Corporal Thurman described the men as "nerved for battle." In a letter to his brother, Private William Thomas expressed the disappointment of everybody in missing the battle for Guayama, as they had been left back at port to unload the ship. They all wanted to get in the fight. If peace came, there would be no glory. Hopefully, their time would come.

The eagerly awaited push to conquer the island came on August 6. The commander of the Puerto Rican Campaign, General Nelson Miles, set in motion four columns to ultimately converge on San Juan.[29] Two columns would march north from Guanica to Arecibo, a port on the coast that was connected to San Juan by rail. Another column would advance on Aibonito, a town situated in the mountains that was about twenty-five miles northwest from Guayama and forty-five miles southwest of San Juan. As for the Fourth OVI and all the other units encamped around Arroyo and Guayama, the plan called for a northward drive over the mountains to confront a large Spanish force that was about eighteen miles away, near the town of Cayey. On August 8, Colonel Coit sent Companies A and C (from Columbus, Ohio) on a scouting mission up a narrow mountain road leading to Cayey. Company A led the column. While rounding a sharp bend in the road, they were suddenly confronted with sustained rifle fire from Spanish soldiers who were dug in among the rocks. They were pinned down. They panicked. An attempt to organize an orderly withdrawal fell apart. Frightened soldiers sprinted back to Guayama, spreading the word that the entire command had been wiped out. Amid the excitement that bit of disconcerting news created, Private Samuel A. Williams kept his cool and rallied Company H into line, ready for action. An officer noticed his calm organization and recommended his promotion to sergeant, which was done. The Spanish did not follow the retreating Americans. For that matter, they were such lousy shots that only five Americans had minor wounds. Those who had not panicked straggled back into camp. The reputations of Companies A and C were seriously wounded. The commander of Company C was accused of cowardice and relieved of his command. He tendered his resignation, which was accepted, and returned to Columbus.

The kickoff for the big battle for Cayey came on August 13. As long as the rumor of peace remained just a rumor, Company H had a chance at its day of glory. The plan called for the First City Troop of Philadelphia (cavalry), the Third Illinois (infantry), the Fourth Pennsylvania (infantry) and an Indiana battery of artillery to march up the narrow road that Companies A and C had made their ignominious retreat down a few days before. Even the band members were ordered to leave their instruments behind and accompany the regiment as medical orderlies. As for Company H, it, along with the rest of the Fourth OVI, was to maneuver to the left and come in behind Spanish entrenchments. Their march was a hard fifteen miles over mountains and ravines that often only allowed soldiers to pass in single file. The sun beat down on them, and they soon began disposing of tents, blankets and ponchos. Some of them dropped from the ranks on account of the heat. They formed up at the bottom of a hill to rest and allow stragglers to catch up. They could see the Spaniards in strong entrenchments about six hundred yards away. There were about 1,500 of them, and they were in a good position to cause Company H serious damage. The coming battle would prove to be the toughest Company H and the Fourth OVI had faced—not that they had exactly been through anything approaching arduous combat. This was their chance to prove their mettle, live up to their bravado and redeem themselves from the embarrassment that Companies A and C had brought down on the regiment five days before. They would have tales of glory to pass on to the next generation, as their Civil War fathers had before them. And their cause was just, as old Civil War Captain Milstead would have said in his speech had he been able to deliver it to Company H the day they departed Portsmouth—"Unforeseen changes in the program prevented him from doing so." Probably to oblige the captain and enlighten the public, the full speech was printed in the *Portsmouth Blade*. The Spanish, he said, are devoid of manhood and humanity. The Chicago major who had come through Camp Thomas told them to "be manly men and Christian soldiers." Local newspapers constantly lionized the bravery and sacrifice of "the boys." All the appeals to patriotism, Christianity and manhood only served to legitimatize something that was already there—they were impatient young men keen to fight and be done. They knew what they had signed up for, and no one backed out.

Their new Krag-Jorgenson rifles were loaded. Extra ammunition was packed in their web belts. The dynamite artillery was sited in on the enemy emplacements. Sweat and excited hearts reduced everything to tunnel vision on attacking the Spaniards' fortified entrenchments. The commanders were within a breath of ordering the attack.

Then, the fickle god of war decided to get involved. In one of those weird juxtapositions of timing and best-laid plans that send a soldier's fate in a wholly different direction, Private Emmett K. McKeown, from twenty miles away, came galloping up on a lathered-up horse that showed hard riding to announce that peace had been declared and that there would be no fighting that day.

Letters home showed two feelings about the cancelled attack—relief from the uncertainty that they might be killed or wounded and frustration that they could not fight and gamble with their lives. Private Harry U. Mohl called the news "glad tidings." But as far as Sergeant Walter H. Trimmer could tell, the men of Company H were "disappointed." Soldier/reporter Private Thurman described the men as "gloomy" over not finally having their battle. But that's how it went; stand down and then march to the rear, back down the difficult terrain, toward Guayama. On their return march, the men got within two miles of Guayama and stopped. They were exhausted. A few scrounged for wood and cooked some slices of bacon. It was nighttime. They laid down on the hard ground and fell asleep. They would finish the trek back to camp the next day.

WAITING TO GO HOME AND...
WAITING TO GO HOME

I t was camp life all over again—sort of. Surely, the men thought, they would not be there for long. After the battle that never was, the men pitched their tents on the outskirts of Guayama and fell into a routine of making the best of the heat and boredom. The rumor was that they would not have to wait long before marching off to San Juan, where they would board a boat to "the sweet land of liberty" and then catch a few trains to Portsmouth. They thought it would be a month at most before they were home. Colonel Coit had requested to depart as quickly as possible, as many of the men were students and needed to get back in time to register for fall classes. Others just needed to get back to their jobs. Their soldier's pay barely allowed their families to scrape by. Some wanted to get back in time for hunting season.

But this was the army. It was October 29 before the men climbed the gangplank of the SS *Sedgwick* and set off on a northern course.[30] By then, another Company H soldier had died of disease in Puerto Rico; one died on a ship that was heading back to the United States (he was buried at sea), and two others who had been sent back earlier died in hospitals. Company H became part of the legacy of the Spanish-American War; more of the company's men died from disease than combat.

Everything about the campsite was undesirable. At that point, the "weapons" of the soldiers were picks and shovels, which they employed to dig sinks on rocky ground and set up tents on hillsides. There was a shortage of wood for cooking. Drill could only be conducted in small units, as there was no open space large or level enough for marching. No one saw the need for it anyway. Since there was no thought that they would be there long, the men slept on the ground. After a while, a few obtained planks to put down floors in their tents. Sometimes, bullets whizzed overhead at night. Apparently, some were still loyal to Spain; they either did not get the word that peace was at hand or just did not care. No one was hurt. Mail from home was scarce and spotty. Some mail from home was still arriving long after Company H departed the island. Newspapers that were days and weeks old were delivered. A creek nearby provided water for bathing and washing clothes until a unit from the Third Illinois camped upstream and began dumping their waste in it. From then on, the men had to carry their water in from the city.

Provisions became an issue. Usually, the only rations furnished by the army were the same kind issued on the day of their departure from Camp Thomas. An occasional issue of rice and potatoes came through. Local markets and individual Puerto Ricans provided some variety, but money was scarce, as the paymaster had not yet appeared in camp. The men were prohibited from eating tropical fruit, as it was felt it would make them thirsty and they would end up drinking contaminated water. Individual shipments from families helped augment the men's diets. To the puzzlement of the soldiers, they found they could use their hardtack to barter for food. The natives seemed to like it. And, of course, there was always "foraging." Still, there was always that peculiar personality in any unit that found hardship and inconvenience almost enjoyable. Company H's Private Evan G. Harris appears to have been that man, as he never got sick and gained weight. His nickname was "Dizzy."

From the very beginning, the soldiers found the local population friendly.[31] Indeed, their first encounter with the Puerto Ricans was one of exuberance. They exalted in their liberation from Spanish control and showed their appreciation of their American liberators by waving, dancing, yelling and hugging and kissing the soldiers. After the natives and soldiers settled down with each other, a few fights broke out, usually over disagreements on purchases of food or other items. Local merchants and women who did laundry raised their prices, displeasing the soldiers. At first, part of a hardtack could get a cigar, then it took a whole hardtack, then two. But on the whole, it was a peaceful occupation. Local officials held banquets for the soldiers. A group of young boys was seen marching through town, waving the American flag and whistling "A Hot Time in the Old Town Tonight." Even Spanish officers who began returning to the city showed considerable deference to the soldiers and would doff their hats whenever they passed the American flag. Individual Puerto Ricans invited soldiers into their homes. Sergeant Newman, Corporal Thurman and Private Mitchell H. Evans were invited by the civil engineer of southern Puerto Rico to visit him. He was described by Thurman as "belonging to the best families of the island." His two daughters played the piano for the men, and the he presented each of them with a cane made out of native wood.

Soldiers' letters home remarked on the beauty of the women and the countryside in general. Some called it paradise. They gave diverse opinions on the people. Some soldiers were racist in their views, but others were more tolerant and curious of local customs. They found the newness of the country personally broadening and appealing. Corporal Searl was not the only one who gave a thought to maybe living there some day.

Any positive or negative feelings about the people and country of Puerto Rico took a back seat to the men's desire to go home. When the health of Company H and the Fourth OVI began to break down, camp life became threatening. It was not just an inconvenience anymore.

The people of Scioto County wanted their soldiers home. They read the newspaper stories of scarce rations that were often inedible. They were alarmed by stories of soldiers dying of diseases, such as typhoid and yellow fever. The death of Daniel Dodge made it real. They knew "the boys" were not immune. People and newspapers began to write letters and editorials. Even the clamor of the soldiers themselves reached hometown readers. The war was over, America won—why are they still there? The Fourth OVI had done the real fighting when it first assaulted Guayama, so they wanted someone else do occupation duty. The Relief Committee, composed of the relatives and friends of Company H, appealed directly to the president to muster the company out immediately. The appeal was denied.

The good and not so good tempo of life back in the "sweet land of liberty" moved on. It was a midterm election year. The Democratic *Portsmouth Daily Times* and the Republican *Portsmouth Blade* provided the local readership with spirited commentary that was completely devoid of even the pretense of objectivity. The personal hostility each editor had for the other and their respective supporters poured from every edition. Even Company H was brought into the fray. The editor of the *Blade* Charles Hard (mockingly called Sister Hard by *Times* editor J.L. Patterson) accused his rival of fomenting the disruption in the unit that lead to the resignations of Captain Pritchard and Lieutenant Pratt. Meanwhile, Patterson accused Hard of not using his political connections to have Company H returned home sooner.

The writing on the reverse of this image reads, "Corporal Chas. W. Reed (seated) & Private Walter H. Stone Portsmouth Boys of Co. H. 4th O.V.I. Taken in Porto [*sic*] Rico with child." *Courtesy of the L.M. Strayer Collection.*

Of course, alongside such spitefulness, the usual daily conversations took place. The Grand Army of the Republic had meetings; the opera house had performances; a checkers club was formed; lodges had officer elections; land was bought and sold; people were arrested; there were accidents, fires and fights; babies were born; and older residents passed away. F.C. Daehler advertised furniture of "artistic design," Marting Bros. & Co. had the largest line of men's underwear and the Arlington Hotel provided meals and beds at all hours. Outlandish claims were made for miracle potions with no thought to truth; $1,000 in gold was promised if a certain medicine did not cure "syphilis, stunted parts, lost manhood, impotency, nervous debility, unnatural discharges, etc." A certain pill was said to cure "wind and pain in the stomach."

National and international news was given ink. Native American uprisings flared up, gold was discovered in the Alaskan Klondike, the French government decided to revisit the espionage trial of Captain Alfred Dreyfus and American soldiers were fighting in the Philippines. Some of the local news struck home personally for some of the members of Company H. The mother of Sergeant George G. Oldfield died, and the police were looking for Al Turner, who had "criminal intercourse" with the thirteen-year-old daughter of his brother Private Joseph Turner.

Just as it had when the company was at Camps Bushnell and Thomas, the hometown did its best to support its boys. The ladies of the Army and Navy League had been busy at All Saints Episcopal Church, putting together a large quantity of supplies for shipment to Puerto Rico. Meticulous thought was given to the best way to get the shipment specifically to Company H. The United States surgeon general George Sternberg told the league to ship the supplies to New York City, where they would be promptly loaded onto a hospital ship that was headed to the island. The supplies went out on September 9, but by October 10, Company H had not received them. It looked like another case of stolen goods, similar to the food baskets that were handed up to soldiers on the wrong train as it passed through Ashland. The ladies were reported to be "very indignant" and were demanding an investigation by the adjutant general of the army Henry Corbin. Company H never received the shipment. Families who sent items to their soldiers individually also found that some of their shipments had disappeared into the unknown abyss of army supply.

Some Company H soldiers began trickling back to the United States due to illness. Privates Armstrong and Johnson had been sent to a hospital back in the United States soon after arriving in Puerto Rico. When the disease caught hold, larger numbers of soldiers were taken off the island. Sergeant Walter H. Trimmer, Privates Duncan M. Douglas, Alexander R. Mead, William I. Edwards, John Youngman, Edward B. Hicks, Harry W. Mathiot, Mathew W. Thompson and Charles E. Hood were shipped out early.[32] Typhoid was the usual malady.

Typhoid is a bacterial infection that begins with contaminated water or food or contact with someone who is infected. The symptoms of a high fever, headache, abdominal pain and either constipation or diarrhea appear gradually, from one to three weeks after contact. It can be fatal. Modern antibiotics have virtually eliminated the disease in industrialized countries, but in an age when such medicine did not exist, it was feared. Quarantine, treating the symptoms and prayer were the best interventions of the day. The afflicted soldiers had to pretty much get well on their own. Dysentery also took a toll. At one Company H assembly, only twenty-seven were able to make formation. Yellow fever and malaria also stalked the soldiers, but typhoid seemed to have been the bane of Company H.

Hospital conditions in Puerto Rico were described as "deplorable."[33] In fact disease and medical treatments throughout the entirety of the Caribbean theater were national scandals. It was a medical disaster for which many felt there was no justification. Hospital staff were overwhelmed, and supplies were short. By the time the government got around to adequately addressing the problem, the sickness had burned itself out.[34] The feeling among the soldiers in the ranks about the military hospital on Puerto Rico was that it was the place to go and die, and many thought it should be avoided. The Red Cross hospital had also been set up and was deemed to be a better facility. The intrepid soldier/reporter Private Patterson for the *Daily Times* had gotten himself court-martialed for reporting on the dreadful conditions Daniel Dodge had to endure before his death. In that earlier dispatch, he had mentioned that the chaplain was enjoying a cigar in a pharmacy when he should have been at the funeral for Private Dodge. When Private Patterson learned that the chaplain was on official duty elsewhere, he admitted his injustice and apologized. In a personal letter home, dated September 12, Patterson reported that his own health was "pretty bad" and that he was "weak as a cat." His father and editor, J.L. Patterson, was sufficiently alarmed by his son's condition that he was able to secure the discharge of young Patterson by simply pointing out that he was under age (seventeen years old) when he enlisted. The senior Patterson left for Puerto Rico to bring his son home. He also took with him a sealed casket to bring home the body of Daniel Dodge. The fathers of Privates Thompson and Mathiot and the brother of Sergeant Trimmer were likewise rushing to Newport News to be at the bedside of their very ill sons and brother.

The other intrepid soldier/reporter Corporal Thurman, writing for the *Portsmouth Blade*, described the poignant scene of a soldier's death and burial in a September 13 dispatch:

> *All that is mortal is carefully wrapped in the American colors and placed in a rude coffin of plain lumber around which is also wrapped the American flag. The coffin, with its unfortunate contents, is lifted into a hearse (which is indeed ancient, being without glass on the sides) and slowly, the procession of a chaplain, colonel, his captain with a military escort moves on toward the last resting place, while the band plays the doleful strains of a funeral march. It is necessary to pass down the principal street in Guayama in order to reach the cemetery. While the funeral procession passes, the American soldier always raises his hat, and often, tears fall from his cheek for his unfortunate comrade. At the grave (which has been dug to a depth of about four feet and the water just bailed out), a parting salute is fired, a short service by the chaplain, and the visitors are requested to report to their company commanders.*

Their graves were marked with wooden boards.

The next Company H soldier to perish was Kurt Sparka.[35] He was from Columbus, Ohio, and had gone over to Camp Bushnell to enlist in the army. He ended up being assigned to Company H. Other than a notice that he had been loaded onto a relief ship headed to the United States and another that told of his subsequent death, no other mention of him appears in Company H letters home or in the Portsmouth newspapers. Any communication from him would have naturally gone to Columbus. He died on October 5 in Pennsylvania Hospital in Philadelphia, Pennsylvania. He was nineteen years old at the time.

Quartermaster Sergeant Charles C. Wilhelm was granted a thirty-day furlough so he could go home and take care of his business. Whatever his business was is unknown. The city directory says he was a clerk. Soldiers were doing their best to get off the island. The most common avenue out was to be very sick. In an uncommon policy of common sense, the army allowed those who recovered stateside to go home rather than return to the island. Private William L. Cole went home early because he accidently shot off one of his toes.

Those who were left had to find something to do. Quaint as Guayama might have been with its old cathedral and its hospitable people, life became boring—very boring. The camp was described in a *Columbus Dispatch* article as "quiet, listless," and the soldiers were said to be "gloomy." There was minimum guard duty, which was lax in execution. There was a limit to the number of interesting seashells one could pick up on the beach. A lot of the men were getting tired of fruit. An unnamed private became drunk in a Guayama bar, foolishly flashed around some money and was promptly robbed. Company M (from Circleville, Ohio) composed a song, which became the anthem of the Fourth OVI:

> *Lying in the guard house, awaiting my discharge—*
> *To H--l with all the officers, the provost and the guard—*
> *When we get back to Circleville, as happy as a clam,*
> *To tell about the sow-belly we ate for Uncle Sam.*
> *Home boys, home, its home you ought to be!*
> *Home, boys, home, in your own country!*
> *Where the ash and the oak and the bonnie willow tree—*
> *Where the grass grows green—in God's country.*

The big event of entertainment and much-needed distraction from the tedium of occupation was the vaudeville show the Fourth OVI put together. The flyer announcing the event read as follows:

4TH OHIO INFANTRY VAUDEVILLE COMPANY
Gauyama Theatre, Puerto Rico
September 13–15, 1898

Company H contributed to the show with Sergeant Samuel A. Williams, who billed himself as a comedian ("the curbside comedian who wants a moment with you"), and Corporal Joseph C. Bratt, who showed off his skills as a gymnast ("difficult feats on horizontal and other bars"). Some "notes" at the end of the flyer gave some sardonic wit to occupation life after the fighting had ceased.

> *Eggs tendered as compliments must be scrambled and not over six weeks old.*
> *The Mint Julep counter to the right as you enter under personal supervision*
> *of Lieut. W.B. McCloud, who is feeling better.*
> *Palm leaf fans furnished by John Trent, 20 centavos.*

The Colonel offers $5 reward for the petrified prayer the Chaplain lost in the attack on Guayama.

N.B. Major Baker will please occupy an amen pew in the synagogue so that he will be able to comprehend the program.

"And the next day it rained" Genl. Order No. 10.

The September 29 edition of the *Daily Times* reprinted an anonymous letter from "one of the brightest members of Company H" about the vaudeville show. General Frederick Grant, with his staff and many Guayama residents, attended. The women were "swell" and "beautiful" and sat up in the gallery drinking wine. When a little Puerto Rican girl who was dolled up in the Stars and Stripes appeared on stage and a Puerto Rican man made a speech about living under the American flag, Spaniards in the audience hissed. The Puerto Ricans shouted out, "Always!"

12

GOODBYE, PUERTO RICO

I t was another month before the Fourth OVI and Company H boarded the ship en masse and headed home. But to get to dockside, the men first had to march to Cayey, the town where they had almost battled the Spaniards in August but were called off at the last minute. On the dark and dreary day of October 6 the men broke camp and marched out through the rain, leaving Guayama behind them. The band played "Dixie," "Marching Through Georgia" and "The Girl I Left Behind Me." They had been on the island and in the general vicinity for sixty-five days. For some soldiers of Company H, it had to have been a poignant departure, as they had grown to like the strange place and its people. And the Puerto Ricans seemed to have reciprocated the relationship. Men and women being, well, men and women, intimacies had to have been developed, but they were never mentioned in the printed letters back home. (One must wonder if the DNA of Company H soldiers and señoritas inhabit Puerto Rico today.)

The men's farewells to the locals must have been genuine. Some Company H soldiers and Puerto Ricans exchanged letters after returning home. Soldiers so sick that they had to be left behind in the division hospital did not make the march. These men were Privates Henry M. Morrison, Forest C. Briggs, Elbert L. Patterson, William C. Sturgill and John W. Shela. The farewells to their stricken comrades with whom they had shared so much must have been deeply heartfelt and made with promises to see them again back in good old Portsmouth. Companies A and E of the regiment were left behind to garrison Guayama.

The rain became a thunderstorm, but the men kept trudging onward. It became so dark they could not see the person in front of them. Sometimes they were strung out single file and had to hold on to the man's poncho ahead of them. They stopped and rested a while at the top of a mountain amid lightning "balls of fire" and peals of thunder. Then it was up and off they went again. On one side of a narrow trail was a steep mountain wall and on the other "a bottomless pit" whence came the sound of a rushing but unseen mountain stream. One errant step could be the death of a soldier. A lightning bug on the rump of the chaplain's horse ahead helped guide the way. Finally the lights of Cayey appeared far below. Two hours later, exhausted and hungry, they staggered into town. The wagon train with their food could not keep up with them over the mountains. The few who had fallen out hobbled in later. Some of them threw themselves down on bags of hay and oats, sleeping so soundly they had not noticed the bags were infested with fleas "as large as New Jersey mosquitos." They rested a day in Cayey after the grueling seventeen-mile march that would be remembered as the hardest, most dangerous thing they did in Puerto Rico. Each knew, though, that every labored step put them that much closer to home.

Their day of rest in Cayey had them saluting the American flag as it was raised over the town square, marching around the plaza and being serenaded by the local native band, which was described as "not in uniform, either as to dress, time, harmony, pitch or chord." A speech was given by Colonel Coit, and the crowd cheered for the "soldados Americanos." Tomorrow the regiment would resume its march to San Juan. Next stop would be the town of Caguas. Wisely, they sent their baggage train ahead of them.

The distance from Cayey to Caguas was about eighteen miles, but fortunately, it was on a relatively level road. Private Harry U. Mohl remarked about the beauty of the landscape they marched through, saying that it reminded him of the grand scenery they viewed on their train ride from Camp Thomas to Newport News. Caguas was decked out in American flags and red, white and blue colors as Company H and the Fourth OVI marched down the street to the plaza. Private Mohl called the town "a credit to the island." The park reminded him of "Sunnyside," Washington Irving's home on the Hudson River. It was October 8 and they were just twenty-two miles from San Juan. He thought they would be home in time to vote.

The men's stay at Gaguas was comfortable. They bedded down in abandoned Spanish barracks, not the hard ground they were accustomed to. The people were hospitable, generous and deemed to be "more intelligent and the businessmen far more reliable than those at Guayama." Four nurses from central Ohio arrived to help care for any of the sick soldiers. They were so highly regarded that they were made honorary members of the regiment. A most pleasant treat was the daily shipment of ice from San Juan, and for the first time in three months, the men had the opportunity to drink a beer.

The regiment fanned out over the area to garrison small villages and show the flag. A small detachment of Company H soldiers was sent to a place called Aguas Buenos. Regular military routines of drill, posting guard and adhering to schedules and protocol were imposed again. Frequent excursions to San Juan were made by the soldiers when they were given leave. Corporals Thurman and McMonigle rode ponies and a train to the city to witness the raising of the American flag over government buildings and Morro Castle, the fortress at the entrance to San Juan Bay. Letters home became few and far between, as the soldiers probably felt there was no need to bother since they would soon be home anyway.

While they were stationed at Gaguas, word reached Company H that death had struck them again. The victim was one of its most popular and well-liked members, Private Elbert L. Patterson, the plucky soldier/reporter for the *Daily Times*. His death hit the company hard. Letters home spoke of the affection they had for their "little Pat," probably the smallest member in the company. Corporal Searl asked his father, Ferdando Searl, a Scioto County probate judge and poet, to compose a poem in honor of his comrade.[36] Private James F. Stewart asked his father to turn to the last paragraph of Charles Dickens's book *David Copperfield* to get a sense of how he felt about his friend's death.[37] They left him at the hospital in Guayama when they departed for Cayey but were under the impression that he was improving. He died on October 16, at eighteen years of age. He was an 1897 graduate of Portsmouth High School. The city directory had him living at 395 East 11 Street, and the *Portsmouth Blade* had his family living at the corner of Washington and Sixth Streets. His father, who had obtained his discharge, had telegraphed his son that he was on his way to take him back home, but he arrived too late to see his son alive. Naturally, he was devastated. While this is perhaps overdramatized, it is still a believable scene of wrenching grief; young Elbert, in his delirium, is reported to have said, "Papa is coming." When his father did come, he found his last telegram pinned to his dead son's jacket. The father returned to New York City and telegraphed ahead that he would be returning to Portsmouth with two bodies, those of Daniel Dodge and his son. Also with him were Corporal Searl and Sergeant Oldfield, who were given furlough to provide what support they could to a shattered father.

The *Sedgwick* appeared in the harbor at Arroyo in the latter part of October, and it took on board Companies A and E. It cruised along the coastline, stopping to pick up other companies of the regiment that were arriving at San Juan Harbor on October 27. As soon as the ship reached Arroyo, word began to spread, and by the next day, Company H and the rest of the Fourth OVI were ready to go. On October 29, at about 4:00 p.m., they boarded. Around dark, the ship raised anchor and slowly started to steam out of the harbor. As it passed, other ships fired salutes, bands played "Yankee Doodle" and "Home Sweet Home" and cheers went up from soldiers and sailors. Just as they had months ago, while pulling away from the United States on the *St. Paul*, the men must have been up against the rails, watching the pageantry and the Puerto Rican landscape fade from view and thinking of home, just a few days away. They were fewer in number, and like all soldiers who have been through a journey into war, their thoughts were subdued. Unlike their southern voyage, they did not have to worry about what unknown experiences awaited them. At the end of this journey, they knew what awaited them—home. The *Sedgwick* made for open sea, and it was set on a northerly course for New York City. It was over. The men's heroic struggle against brutish Spain was at an end and was summarized rather unceremoniously by the *Daily Times* in an October 27 editorial that read, in part, "Co. H didn't kill many Spaniards, but they frightened them into prompt surrender."

13

HOME

A soldier in Company K died and was buried at sea. For Company H, the voyage was uneventful but for a storm the third night out. The ship was smaller than the *St. Paul* and more crowded, but the food was much improved. A few days in, some distant hills and church steeples appeared on the far horizon. One can imagine how the soldiers must have rushed to the rails eager to see their homeland. The band struck up patriotic tunes, and the soldiers went wild with joy. They cheered and strained to get a glimpse of the United States. Steaming ever northward, the *Sedgewick* eased past Sandy Hook, New Jersey, the gateway to New York's Hudson Bay. There, the ship had to anchor at a designated quarantine station until it had to be inspected and cleared before it could proceed into the harbor.[38] The men spent the night on board and woke in a thick fog in the morning. The inspecting officer came on board and began his inspection. It must have been exasperating waiting for him to give his decision. He had to go through the ship and consider the condition of the men and horses on board. There had to have been an uneasy thought that he might make them stay in quarantine and endure another uncertain inspection. Finally, he emerged and, undoubtedly to the relief of all, granted the *Sedgewick* permission to proceed. It eased onward and anchored at the base of the Statue of Liberty, waiting for the fog to clear. One can only imagine their feelings as they gazed up at that imposing symbol of liberty. The fog gave up around noon, and they were able to dock at Jersey City, New Jersey. A train was waiting for them, but as it was not going to leave until midnight, they were granted leave time. Many of the men took a ferry over to New York City, where they went silly, ordering large meals of foods they could not get in Puerto Rico; oysters, apples, butter, pies and fresh bread delighted their palates. After seeing the sights and stuffing themselves, they loaded up bags and baskets with enough to feed an army. At midnight, the train pulled out headed down the B&O Line to Washington, D.C. Perhaps the hypnotic rhythm of the train lulled some of them to sleep. Perhaps others were too excited to sleep. The account of Sergeant Major Charles E. Creager suggests there was great excitement among the Fourth OVI as a whole. They all knew this was their first night on the soil of their country and the coming end of an extraordinary adventure. But first, they had to meet the president.

They arrived in Washington, D.C., shortly after daylight; there, they ate breakfast, stacked arms and then formed up to march in review past President William McKinley, who was standing on the White House terrace. Afterward, and perhaps because they were fellow Ohioans, the president received them inside the East Room of the White House. They were reportedly the only regiment to be hosted in this manner. The president singled out First Sergeant Russell Newman to mention that he knew his nephew in Portsmouth, James Newman. At some point during the day, the regiment formed up on the steps of the United States

The Fourth Ohio Volunteer Infantry Regiment in front of the U.S. Treasury Building in Washington, D.C., after its return from Puerto Rico. *Courtesy of the Southern Ohio Museum and Cultural Center, Portsmouth, Ohio.*

Treasury Building for a photograph. Around 5:00 p.m., the men were back on the train for a nighttime trip across the Allegheny Mountains. At daylight, on a cold, frosty November day, they crossed into Ohio. Some cheered and sang songs—some cried.

Not on the train with their comrades were Company H soldiers who were in the hospital in Newport News. The October 12 edition of the *Portsmouth Blade* printed their names and conditions. They made their homecoming to Columbus on a hospital train.

> *Walter M. Trimmer, malarial fever, condition good.*
> *Mathew W. Thompson, malarial fever, very weak from voyage, prospects for recovery are good.*
> *John Youngman, fever, now convalescent.*
> *Duncan M. Douglas, in good condition.*
> *Edward B. Hicks, convalescent, ready for furlough.*
> *Charles E. Hood, convalescent.*
> *Harry W. Matthiot, very weak, but conditions for his recovery are good.*

Long before Company H left Puerto Rico, the devoted citizens of Portsmouth began preparing for their return. Committees of various organizations were popping up everywhere. Officers were elected, and plans were made. The eagerness to do something distinctive that would honor "the boys" became a sacred duty. Fraternal organizations, such as the Masons and Odd Fellows, met at the Pythian Hall on the southeast corner of Washington and Fourth Streets to consolidate their efforts. An executive committee of former members of Company H met to plan a parade and military ball. This committee soon came to be acknowledged as the leading committee, and all others deferred to it. The editor of the *Portsmouth Blade*, Charles Hard, was elected its chairman. On the subcommittee for parade arrangements was Robert Stanley Pritchard, and on the subcommittee for decorations was Kinney Funk. A delegation was formed to travel to Columbus to coordinate train schedules and the length of time Company H would be in that city. Another delegation coordinated with a Columbus committee to see that the Company H soldiers who were returning on the separate hospital train were transferred and sent home as soon as possible. The women of the DAR, Army and Navy League, Women's Relief Corps and "other ladies" formed a committee to plan a banquet and reception. A writer for the *Daily Times* advised the girls of Portsmouth to get their "kissing apparatus in working order," for "Johnny will soon come marching home." All the town's citizens, including churches, high schools and "colored citizens," were invited and encouraged to take part in welcoming home "the gallant boys." Homes and store fronts were encouraged to decorate with the national colors. Poems were written, songs were sung and church sermons were given in their honor. The *Daily Times* printed the names of the factories that agreed to close and sound their whistles when the company paraded from the train station to lower Market Street and then back up to their armory, where they would be dismissed. The community pulled together to make the homecoming for its boys "the greatest celebration ever seen." The grand marshal for the parade was old Captain Milstead of the Grand Army of the Republic.

Amid the excited planning for the homecoming were the somber arrangements for the funerals and burials of Elbert Patterson and Daniel Dodge. The train bearing their bodies arrived in Portsmouth on Saturday, October 29, at 4:50 a.m. in the morning darkness. Ex-members of Company H took charge. The remains of Daniel Dodge were taken directly to Greenlawn Cemetery and deposited in a vault. Those of Elbert Patterson were taken to Daehler's Mortuary and then moved to his parents' home on the corner of Sixth and Washington Streets.

That Sunday afternoon, a detail of ex–Company H soldiers, GAR veterans, high school pupils and the River City Band escorted Elbert Patterson's body to Bigelow Church. One report said nearly 1,800 crowded inside the church, with many others forced to stand outside in the cold wind. It was said to be the largest crowd ever assembled at a Portsmouth church. Muffled sobs and visible tears were evident. Last rites for Daniel Dodge and Elbert Patterson began promptly at 2:00 p.m., with the high school glee club singing "Rock of Ages." Scripture was read. A song composed by the rector of All Saints Church was sung. Far-ranging eulogies by the pastors of First and Second Presbyterian Churches were given, which, taken together, cited the American Civil War, the Tai Ping Rebellion in China, a Russian battle in Turkestan, Napoleon, Grant, Sherman, Marcus Aurelius, Rome, Lincoln, Charles Dickens and passages from the Bible. Whitcomb Riley's poem "Away" was read. Pictures of the two dead boys were framed in floral wreaths.

At the end of the service, Elbert Patterson's casket was escorted to Greenlawn Cemetery and placed in the vault. Many stood silently on sidewalks as a long line of carriages followed the cortege. His remains were later taken to McConnelsville, Ohio, and buried beside his mother's grave. The casket of Daniel Dodge was taken from the cemetery vault to the Dodge family lot. An immense number of floral offerings covered both caskets. At the base of a column of white roses and chrysanthemums for Elbert was the number "30," which, in newspaper parlance of the day, signified "end of message" on a telegraphic news dispatch. The bugler sounded taps as Daniel's casket was lowered into the ground. The early October evening crept over the cemetery, ending the proceedings. A solemn reverence descended over the city.

Adding to the city's collective grief was a notice received by the parents of Henry M. Morrison that said their son, age twenty, died on board the hospital ship *Missouri* on October 26 and was buried at sea "with full military honors." The last message they had received from Henry's officers had given them hope that he was convalescing from typhoid fever. He was a country boy born on the family farm in Nile Township, and he received his education at the Elm Tree School. He moved to East Ninth Street in Portsmouth with his parents and worked in a shoe factory for a while before becoming a salesman. He was on the local football team and had already been a member of Company H for four years when war was declared on Spain.

It seems he was well liked by all his comrades. Although word of his death was received before the funeral services of Elbert Patterson and Daniel Dodge, newspaper accounts of the eulogies do not show that his name was mentioned. It was left to ex-members of Company H to memorialize their fallen compatriots. At a separate meeting, a memorial statement adopted by them was published by the *Portsmouth Blade* on November 2 to honor Daniel Dodge, Kurt Sparka, Elbert Patterson and Henry Morrison. It read, in part, "[They] gave up home and kindred and the bright hopes and aspirations that greet young men at the entrance of manhood. They each believed their selfish interests were subservient to the country's cause of liberty and humanity."

The celebration for the living members of Company H went forward with passion. The city vibrated with excitement over the anticipated return of "the boys." The long, crowded procession of parade entrants was organized, their spots in the line and starting points were designated. Oscar Newman, Benjamin Bratt and J.J. Spencer would go to Columbus to meet the train carrying Company H and accompany them back to Portsmouth. A series of whistle blasts from the waterworks helped the residents track their progress. Fifteen blasts meant the train had left Columbus, one blast indicated the homebound train had reached Circleville, two blasts meant they had reached Chillicothe, three blasts meant they had reached Waverly and four blasts

DANIEL H. DODGE.
[PAGE 256.]

FORREST BRIGGS.
[PAGE 257.]

HENRY M. MORRISON.
[PAGE 257.]

ELBERT PATTERSON.
[PAGE 256.]

MEMBERS OF CO. E, 4TH O. V. I., SPANISH–AMERICAN WAR
LOST THEIR LIVES IN THE SERVICE.

Pictured are four of the five Company H soldiers from Scioto County who died. The fifth was Kurt Sparka [sic] (Sparks) of Columbus. The erroneous designation of Company E in the caption of the photograph occurred when the company was mustered into federal service. Local pressure reverted the designation back to Company H. *This image was taken from* History of Scioto County, Ohio, *by Nelson W. Evans, Portsmouth, Ohio, 1903.*

signaled that they had reached Big Run. At the final signal, all the schools were to be dismissed. By then, the train would have been forty minutes away. Parade participants had to quickly form up at Second and Market Streets, march to Waller and then north to the train station, where they waited for their soldiers. All were instructed to wear a small American flag pinned to their lapel. Police had orders to arrest anyone who was crowding too close to the line of march.

That Sunday morning, November 6, the train carrying the Fourth OVI pulled into Columbus. The Columbus reception that was given to the regiment was as grand as the one that was planned for Company H in Portsmouth. "A mass of humanity" greeted the train. A large parade proceeded from the B&O Station to an auditorium, "where a bountiful spread had been prepared by the ladies of Columbus." Afterward, they signed muster rolls in order to receive their next pay. In addition to the welcoming committee of Newman, Bratt and Spencer, a certain Judge Ball, who was running for reelection, also went north to glad-hand his soldier constituents. He was lampooned in the *Daily Times*.

Around 8:00 a.m. on a sunny Monday, the waterworks let loose fifteen whistle blows. Company H was leaving Columbus and was only five hours away. After unloading Company M and its baggage in Circleville, there was one toot of the waterworks whistle, then two, then three, then four. They were forty minutes from the station. The parade participants hurriedly formed up on the lower end of Market Street, with the police leading off and old Grand Marshal Captain Milstead and his GAR following. Following him was the River City Band, led by their drum major, none other than Frank B. Pratt, the former lieutenant of Company H (who resigned at Camp Thomas) who subsequently became the drum major of the Fourth Kentucky Volunteer Infantry. He wore his officer's uniform. A couple of units back, a formation of ex–Company H soldiers was led by none other than Captain Robert Stanley Pritchard (who also resigned at Camp Thomas). In their descriptions of the parade, neither the *Daily Times* nor the *Portsmouth Blade* mentioned the presence of Kinney Funk anywhere. Altogether, there were at least twenty-one official entrants in the procession to welcome the boys home and many others who spontaneously stepped into or drove carriages into the street, adding to the traffic. With flag-waving folks from county and city, the crowd was as immense as it had been the day they sent the boys off over six months before.

One can imagine the rowdiness and excitement of the soldiers on the train. Singing, laughing, joking and the youthful air of young men must

The return of Company H, marching west on Second Street. The horses and buggies in the lower-right corner were sitting where the Washington Hotel was eventually built. *Courtesy of the Southern Ohio Museum and Cultural Center, Portsmouth, Ohio.*

have rocked the passenger cars as much as the rails did. Perhaps a few others were quietly lost in thought. One of the soldiers stuck his head out the train window and spied the Cincinnati, Portsmouth and Virginia Railroad bridge that crossed the Scioto River. Familiar landmarks stoked their excitement. The engineer opened up the train whistle all the way in. The conductor walked through the aisle announcing the next stop— "Portsmouth." One of the soldiers, unable to restrain himself, jumped from the train and hurried to his house. The excitement must have been near riotous. Crowded in the passenger cars were some of the "souvenirs" they had dragged back—dogs, fighting chickens and rum. Not on the train was Artificer Donaldson, who had made it as far as Columbus but was so sick that he was taken to a hospital. He recovered and joined his family later.

The train pulled into the Norfolk and Western Depot. No one was there. The crowds were waiting at the CP&V Depot, so again, the engineer hit the whistle, let go the steam and chugged down to the right place. It must have been pandemonium with the shriek of steam and the clanging of the train bell amid the crush of friends and loved ones rushing to the passenger cars, trying to touch their soldiers amid the cacophony of every steam whistle and church bell in the city and the barking and crowing from souvenir dogs and chickens. The baggage was unloaded, and soldiers poured out of the cars and pushed their way through the crowd to form up in formation at their place in the parade.

The boys were tanned from the Puerto Rican sun and had lost weight. Like all soldiers who go to the indefinite and then come back to the familiar, they marched with a leanness in their step. Gone was the military stiffness of formation they had had on that April day they left for war. Gone was any need to hide trepidations with bravado. They were with their comrades in arms on home ground, surrounded by those who loved them.

They marched down Waller Street to Second Street, then over to Market Street to swing around the center esplanade, then back on Second Street to Chillicothe Street and up to their armory. Crowds cheered and waved flags. Captain Smith read orders from Colonel Coit, placing the company on furlough for sixty days, and then he announced the Grand Opera House would put on the war drama *Darkest Russia*. Front-row seats were reserved for those in uniform. Then they were dismissed, told to take care of their rifles and return in about an hour to pick up their baggage. They were home.

14

AND THEN...

E verywhere they went, they were welcomed home and honored. Assemblies of the fraternal societies praised them, church sermons were given in admiration of their service, poems and songs were composed for them and receptions and banquets were held for them. A lavish banquet was given at Seel's Hall, which was decorated with flags, bunting, flowers and autumn leaves; it featured raw and escalloped oysters, turkey, cheese, bread, fruit, ice cream and cake, and it was all topped off with bonbons and cigars.[39] Four empty chairs were reserved for the company's deceased comrades. Then, they proceeded over to Dice's Hall, where they received the citizens of the community who had come to welcome them home.[40] Even a steady rain did not stifle the large turnout. Speeches were delivered extoling the troops' bravery and the glorious reputation that Company H had brought to Scioto County. Mementoes, badges and banners were conferred on the company. A week later, another reception given by the King's Daughters of Second Presbyterian Church featured a literary and musical program. The Sanford, Storrs and Varner Clothing and Furnishings Store gave them a 10 percent discount.

In gratitude for all that was showered on them, the company published a statement in the *Daily Times* that said they would endeavor to be "good, loyal, upright citizens." They also put together a skit of what camp life was like. Every facet of "real camp life" was reenacted on stage so that the folks at home could know what their boys had gone through. The presentation at the Grand Opera House was wildly popular. It was advertised, "Think of it! A trip to Porto Rico for 50, 35 and 25 cents. Spend a day in camp with Company H. You will never have another opportunity to see the daily routine of a soldier's life." From reveille to taps, the soldiers pitched tents, lined up for roll call, stood guard, ate meals, paraded and did the things that soldiers did. Drill of the "awkward squad" and soldiers carrying away buckets of quinine (used to treat malaria) from sick call provoked howls of laughter. In between scenes, patriotic songs were performed. Two hundred little girls dressed in red, white and blue stood in a flag formation. A curious part of the program was called "Porto Ricans Sell Candy." This was no masquerade. No one dressed up or pretended to be Puerto Ricans. Three Puerto Rican boys who had followed the company all through Puerto Rico had also followed it back to Portsmouth. Two participated in the show. The skit, which was meant to be as realistic as the soldiers could make it on stage, had the Puerto Rican boys robbed of their candy and tossed high in blankets. They lived with Harvey Wills, Tod Wilhelm and Ralph Calvert, apparently without disruption to their households. The boy living with Ralph Calvert was named Josa Pagau, and he became critically sick with "quick consumption." The last report about him said he was improving. The boy living with Harvey Wills was named B. Senta Soto, and he was about twelve years old.[41] The three Puerto Rican youngsters became quite a curiosity. Townspeople would come by to simply look at them. It was reported that a plot by "two low characters" to kidnap two of them and use them as an attraction in a museum had been thwarted.

Not everything was so rosy for Company H. Private David J. Johnson got himself thrown in jail after being drunk and disorderly. A week after returning home, the father of Sergeant Foster died. It also seemed that the conniving and personality clashes that plagued the company away from home carried on after returning. Some hated Colonel Coit, while others did not. It was reported in the *Daily Times* that threats had been made against him to keep him from attending the official military ball that was planned for Christmas Eve. Security measures were taken by the mayor and police to keep the colonel safe. On the night of the ball, he was reported to have been "nervous" while giving a lengthy speech that received scattered applause. In a totally different spin by the *Portsmouth Blade*, there were no concerns with the colonel's visit. The paper reported that everything was calm and normal as he made his appearance at various venues around the city. The partisan views of the colonel and everything else associated with Company H continued to sour the celebratory air far into the Christmas season.

Kendall's Hall at the southeast corner of Chillicothe and Seventh Streets was secured for the official military ball, where relics brought back from Puerto Rico were displayed, including—it was alleged—the sword of Ponce de Leon from when he was on the island looking for the fountain of youth. Proceeding the opening of the ball was the Grand March, led by one of the Puerto Rican boys carrying the Spanish flag and an American carrying the American flag. An invited guest, Chaplain Schindel of Circleville, created a stir when he said dancing was something that men and women could enter into and come away as "pure" as they had been when they began. Then, he tried a few rusty steps himself. A separate ball that was planned by some enlisted men came to naught when it was determined that they intended to keep most of the proceeds from ticket sales to themselves.

An unexplained petition was taken up and sent to Governor Bushnell. It opposed the promotion of Sergeant Williams to second lieutenant. He was the man who was promoted for rallying the troops when Companies A and C were ambushed; he was also the comedian in the vaudeville show that the regiment put together when they were on the island. Why he was unpopular with some of his mates is unknown. The petition was initiated by Private James Skelton at a Company H assembly, and it apparently garnered a fair number of signatures. The supporters of Williams and those who opposed him were said to have made the meeting "a warm time." Apparently, the governor listened to the detractors of Sergeant Williams, as the official roster listed him as a sergeant instead of a lieutenant when he was mustered out.

Despite the celebrations, speeches and shenanigans that were inspired by Company H's arrival, death was not finished with the company. A six-foot-tall, blue-eyed young man with dark hair and a dark complexion named Forest C. Briggs died at Fort Hamilton General Hospital in New York City on November 10. The community again reeled with grief. His death was all the more dreadful because the last reports of his convalescence had been positive. Raised on the family farm in Clay Township, he had worked as a stenographer at the N&W Railway Office. He had been a member of Company H since 1892 and was quite popular with his mates, advancing to the rank of first sergeant by the time war was declared. Soon afterward, he was given a commission as a second lieutenant. He soon fell sick though and was unable to perform his duties. His father rushed to New York to be at his son's side and was able to spend a week with him before he died.

His body arrived at the C&O Depot in South Portsmouth, Kentucky, on the evening of November 12, a Saturday. The coffin was accompanied across the river to his parents' home on Chillicothe Pike by soldiers and ex-soldiers of Company H and a contingent of the GAR. The scene for young Briggs was virtually as it had been two weeks earlier for Patterson and Dodge. The next day, in the rain, his body was taken to the Sixth Street Methodist Episcopal Church, where a large crowd was already packed inside. Hundreds who were wrapped as warmly as possible stood with their umbrellas outside in the cold rain. The eulogy was given over the coffin, which was surrounded with wreaths.

At the conclusion of the service, the slow march to Greenlawn Cemetery began, with the River City Band playing its solemn strains. It was followed by the hearse, the pallbearers and a long line of carriages. A hush fell over the crowd that was watching the cortege. Many heads were made bare, and flags drooped from windows. Hundreds were waiting at the cemetery. The procession slowly wound its way over a gently curving pathway to a tent that was covering the burial site piled high with floral tributes. As the body of Forest Briggs was lowered into the ground, a firing squad squeezed off three volleys, followed by the lingering sound of taps as it was played out on a Spanish bugle. Absent from the crowd was Colonel Coit. It was rumored his request to attend was denied by the family. Then, the vast crowd melted away into the drizzling, darkening twilight.

15

FADE AWAY

T he boys of Company H visited family, friends and sweethearts;
coped with the good and bad that had happened while they
were gone; caroused and got drunk; recuperated from sickness;
connected with their former employers; and generally delighted in their
notoriety. A few may have revisited Jennie Matthews's "house of bad
repute," which was still in business on West Eleventh Street, just as it
had been when they departed for war. Many of them returned to the
same jobs they had left a little over six months earlier. Many of them went
hunting; some, it seemed, just to disappear into the woods. For those who
voted in the November 8 election, they saw the Republicans humiliate the
Democrats. The holiday season was coming on; it was time to think about
Thanksgiving and Christmas. Merchants began advertising discounts.
Levi York was rebuilding his steel mill on the east end of New Boston,
in an area he named Yorktown. Right beside it, a dandy park with many
wonderful attractions was going up; he called it Millbrook Park. Lieutenant
Smith officially received his captaincy commission. Word was received
that Company H would be officially mustered out of federal service on
January 20, 1899. The men would need to form up one more time, travel
to Columbus January 5, collect their last pay as soldiers in the service of
the United States and become a national guard unit again—Company H
of the Fourteenth Ohio Volunteer Infantry. They were told to take an extra
blanket. Officially, the command of Company H could have been turned
over to First Lieutenant Frank B. Pratt, who had resigned back at Camp

Thomas from federal service but not the Ohio National Guard. Captain Pritchard, apparently deciding to sever all ties with military life, tendered his resignation, effective for both federal and state service, and focused his life on selling and repairing bicycles and selling Welsbach gas heaters.[42] Captain Smith received a crate of the national guard uniforms the company had exchanged for federal uniforms at Camp Bushnell. They would change back to their national guard uniforms when they were mustered out of federal service. Also received by the company quartermaster Sergeant Charles Wilhelm were three heavy boxes of hardtack, which the men were to survive on while waiting in Columbus for their official mustering out.

The Army and Navy League finally received word on the large quantity of supplies they had so diligently packed and shipped to their soldiers while they were still in Puerto Rico. A private in charge of the storeroom in Ponce, Puerto Rico, sent them a letter saying he had found a large box full of broken jars of jellies and wanted to know if the league wanted them back. This probably had the effect of reigniting the initial indignation the league had felt when it had first learned the shipment had disappeared into the murky river of army supply. The private did return a personal letter that the mother of Henry Morrison had mailed to the surgeon of the Fourth OVI in regard to the health of her son.

Company H soldiers who were in the hospital and unable to come on the train with the unit began to recuperate so they could be released. A Puerto Rican dog that had been brought home by Albert Barber was stolen. A telephone line was laid across the Ohio River, connecting Portsmouth and South Portsmouth, Kentucky. The first snow of the winter came two days after Thanksgiving.

For a while, the *Daily Times* and *Portsmouth Blade* continued their bare-knuckled editorial fight with each another. A change of heart came though when the editor of the *Daily Times* J.L. Patterson severed his ties with the paper. Dealing with the death of his son Elbert was naturally a burden, quashing any aspiration he had to carry on as before. There were too many reminders of his boy everywhere. He was also not from Scioto County, and his son was to be buried beside his wife's grave in McConnelsville, Ohio. He had a job interview with a newspaper in Findlay, Ohio. In announcing his departure, Patterson took a parting shot at his rival, stating that, when he had first taken over, he had "found the opposition strong, vulgar and vicious," but from the efforts made over the last six years, he said, "We leave it weak, hypocritical and vain." Graciously, the response of the *Portsmouth Blade* was an olive branch. It wished the new owners success and described them as "able…bright…[and] pleasant." The new owners of the *Daily Times* called their coming editorship "a new era."

Honorifics for Company H tapered off. The Christmas Eve military ball seemed to have been the last major blast of good cheer for Company H. The community they had left over six months earlier embraced them fondly on their return. Some muddled through, but most, as they had promised, became "good, loyal, upright citizens." A veterans' organization was formed. Company H became the Peerless Camp No. 79 and held its meetings in the basement of the Portsmouth Public Library. Soldiers began submitting applications for pensions. Veterans who took the civil service examination were given extra points. A small plaque honoring them was attached to the main flagpole at Camp Oyo, the Boy Scout camp. Soldiers were given the option of purchasing their Krag-Jorgenson military rifles for seventeen dollars. On April 25, 1899, a train carrying a huge gun that had been on the Spanish cruiser *Admirante Oquendo* stopped in Portsmouth to give people an opportunity to gaze on a war trophy. It had been donated to the City of Cincinnati.[43]

War slogged on in the Philippines, where Americans drove out the Spanish only to end up fighting a guerrilla war against Philippine insurgents who were just as unhappy with the prospect of American rule as they had been with Spanish rule. Some of Scioto County's young men in the

A railcar with a cannon from the Spanish cruiser *Maria Theresa* that was presented to Cincinnati by the government stopped in Portsmouth to let the residents look at the spoils of war. *From the* Portsmouth Blade, *April 22, 1899.*

military—but not Company H—found themselves traipsing through an Asian jungle, the first of a generation of others to come.[44]

Another local connection to the Philippine War were the ties a prominent Portsmouth family had to a participant in that fight. Jacob H. Smith grew up in Scioto County, and at an early age, he began a military career. He fought in the Civil War, Indian Wars and, as a lieutenant colonel, the Spanish-American War. In the latter, he was seriously wounded in the Battle of Santiago, Cuba. His bravery in battle was noted in military reports and newspapers. He was the brother-in-law of Judge James W. Bannon, who escorted him to Portsmouth, where he continued to convalesce from his wounds. In 1901, he was a brigadier general in the Philippines. He was recklessly outspoken, saying that he would not respect flags of truce, and he ordered his troops to shoot all insurgents on the spot. His nickname was "Hell Roaring Jake." When given the mission of pacifying the Philippine island of Samar, his orders to his subordinates were simple: kill males ten years or older and turn the place into a "howling wilderness." Only the restrained conduct of a subordinate kept the Samar Campaign from being a bloodbath. At his court-martial, he was convicted of "conduct to the prejudice of good order and military discipline" and forced to retire.

CONCLUSION

I n 1898, the war with Spain gripped the headlines. In an eruption of
patriotic zeal, Americans rushed to the aid of Cuban independence,
equating that struggle against Spain with their own against Great
Britain a little more than a century before. The young men who marched
away to Cuba, Puerto Rico and the Philippines read their history books and
absorbed the story of America's birth. Some had fathers who had read of the
death of the last surviving veteran of the Revolutionary War in 1869. They
were not that far removed from the War of 1812 and the Mexican War, and
they heard the personal firsthand stories from their fathers about the Civil
War. Filled with patriotism, war stories and the fascination that young men
have for fighting, Americans rallied to the Cuban cause. The few pacifist
exceptions—Mark Twain among them—were pushed to the sidelines.

The year saw the United States become a global presence. In Cuba,
Puerto Rico, Guam, Wake Island and the Philippines, the Spanish flag was
replaced with the Stars and Stripes. The door to the American Century
opened. The people of Scioto County, Ohio, and their young soldier boys
joined the show, stepping over the threshold that separated the past and the
future, the old and the new. Whether any of them saw the big picture of the
emerging American empire or not, they were nonetheless proud people who
either answered the call to the colors or enthusiastically supported those who
did. Less than twenty years after that April day, when Company H marched
to the train station at the corner of Tenth and Waller Streets, Americans
were pulled into a monstrous European war that killed millions, including

thousands of Americans. Some who had watched Company H march away in 1898 marched away themselves in 1917. At least two Company H soldiers marched with them.[45] On the war memorial wall in Tracy Park, which borders Chillicothe Street, are the names of the eighty-four Scioto County soldiers who died in that war.

Much changed in 1898. In his book titled *1898*, David Traxel described the year as "the tumultuous year of victory, invention, internal strife, and industrial expansion." It was one of those "rare years" that changed the course of American history. The 1890s was an "uncertain time when anything seemed possible." Scioto County, seated as it was at the confluence of two major rivers and the terminus of competing railroad lines, was swept along in this "uncertain time." By 1898, the enormous social and economic changes of the decade had made their mark on Scioto County— but more was to come. Automobiles, silent movies and "flying machines" were just around the corner. In the prosecution of a European war that was flaring up, the simple rifles and dynamite guns that were familiar to Company H were replaced by mass-killing machine guns, poison gas, aero planes and tanks.

The last surviving veteran of the Spanish-American War died in the early 1990s. But there was controversy over who was last. The last Scioto County resident was gone before then. That may have been Robert Waddell Sr., who died in 1968. Of the grave markers that contain a date of death, his appears to be the last. A survey of cemeteries in Scioto County counted sixty-eight graves of Spanish-American War veterans. One of them was a female nurse, Clara M. Moore, who was buried in the Old South Webster Cemetery, South Webster, Ohio. Not all who were buried in Scioto County were from Scioto County, as some had settled there later (Appendix C).

Newspapers that reported on the celebrations that were held when soldiers left and returned invariably described the experiences as so moving and momentous that they would be remembered "for all time." The reality was exactly the opposite. Epic historical events all but smothered the memory of that "splendid little war." A contemporary national organization, the Sons of Spanish-American War Veterans, attempts to keep the war in the spotlight. A group photograph of its 2018 national convention in Knoxville, Tennessee, shows eighteen attendees. As of May 2016, forty-six children and forty-two widows of Spanish-American War veterans were receiving benefits. The Ohio Department of the United Spanish War Veterans was active into the early 1960s.

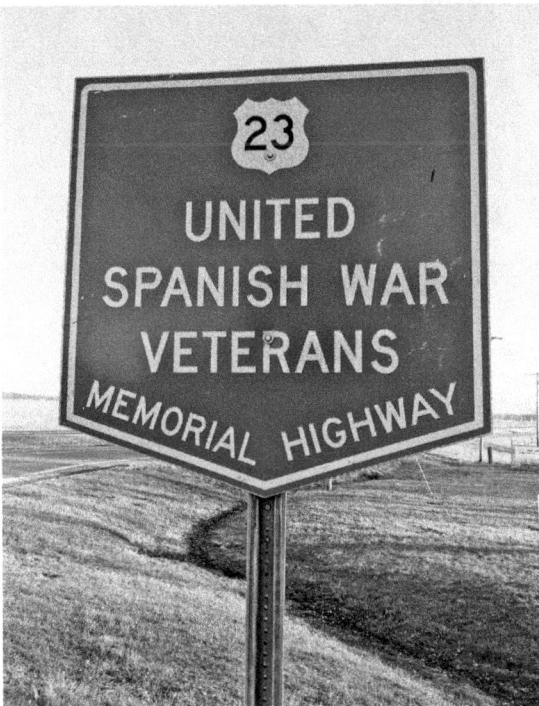

Above: A small plaque was affixed to the flagpole at Camp Oyo Boy Scout Camp in Scioto County in 1930. Peerless Camp No. 79 was the local chapter for Spanish War veterans. It held its meetings in the basement of the Portsmouth Public Library. *Photograph taken by the author.*

Left: State Route 23 from Toledo, Ohio, to Portsmouth was dedicated to veterans of the Spanish War. Signs like this were erected at roadside rest areas. This sign is located at the rest stop north of South Bloomfield. Another was located at the rest stop in Scioto County, just south of the Pike County line, but it is gone now. *Photograph taken by the author.*

Above: Pictured is the author next the memorial to the Fourth Ohio Volunteer Infantry in the plaza in Guayama, Puerto Rico. The names of the five Company H members who died are on the bronze plaque. *Photograph taken by the author's wife, Mary McHenry.*

Opposite: This is a group photograph of Company H in Tracy Park after their return. *Courtesy of Southern Ohio Museum and Cultural Center, Portsmouth, Ohio.*

In Scioto County, the last meeting of the local veterans' organization appears to have taken place in the 1950s. The small plaque affixed to the main flagpole at the Boy Scout camp is still there. State Route 23, which bisects Ohio from Toledo to Portsmouth, was dedicated to the veterans of the "Spanish War." Blue signs were erected at rest stops stating this dedication. It is probably a puzzlement to modern drivers who might ask themselves, "What Spanish War?" The sign at the rest stop on Route 23 just inside Scioto County, where traffic crosses over the Pike County line, was there as recently as a couple of years ago, but it is now gone.

In the city of Guayama, Puerto Rico, a memorial plaque was affixed to a concrete block in the town square; it reads, in part:

Dedicated to the
MEMORY
Of the boys of the Fourth Ohio Vol.
Infantry who lost their lives in
the performance of their duty
in the war with Spain

The names of Daniel H. Dodge, Kurt Sparka, Elbert L. Patterson, Henry M. Morrison and Forest C. Briggs are on that plaque.

The houses, buildings, schools, shops, factories, mills, wagons, carriages, horses, sights, sounds and smells of 1898 are mostly gone and the people who lived in, with and around them all dead. The zeal of tearing things down in order to put up a replacement or just leave a vacant lot kept its grip on Portsmouth, a policy that sadly still exists. Some street names, business names and a ditch remind us of those who marched away to exotic, "dreamlike" Puerto Rico: Kinney's Lane, Calvert's Boulevard, Shela Boulevard, Mathiot Street, Coles Boulevard, Herm's Florist, Distel Construction, Patterson Paper and Funk's Gut—to name a few.

In Appendices A and B are the names of the young men and one woman from Scioto County who went far away in 1898—not all came back. Read their names, and don't forget them.

APPENDIX A

Roster of Company H of the Fourth Ohio Volunteer Infantry Regiment as Printed in Sergeant Major Charles E. Creager's *The Fourteenth Ohio National Guard—The Fourth Ohio Volunteer Infantry*

(Addresses and occupations taken from the 1897 and 1899 Portsmouth City Directory.)

Name	Rank When Mustered Out	Residence/ Occupation	Comment
Robert S. Pritchard	Captain	13 East Eighth Street, Portsmouth, Ohio/bicycle shop owner	He was discharged before unit left for Puerto Rico.
James A. Smith	Captain	Contractor	He assumed command from Pritchard. He was the only Company H officer remaining after Funk was stripped of his rank.

Name	Rank When Mustered Out	Residence/ Occupation	Comment
Frank B. Pratt	First Lieutenant	72 East Fourth Street/ paper hanger	He resigned his commission.
Kinney P. Funk	First Lieutenant	Mount Tabor Road, Portsmouth, Ohio/clerk	He assumed command from Lieutenant Pratt. His muster in and out records state that Funk was a lawyer.
Russell C. Newman	First Sergeant	Stenographer	
Charles C. Wilhelm	Quartermaster Sergeant	19 East Second Street, Portsmouth, Ohio/clerk	
Andrew B. Foster	Sergeant	13 West Ninth Street, Portsmouth, Ohio/clerk	
Walter H. Trimmer	Sergeant	34 East Third Street, Portsmouth, Ohio/shoe cutter	
Samuel A. Williams	Sergeant	28 East Ninth Street, Portsmouth, Ohio/shoe worker	
George G. Oldfield	Sergeant	Student	
Monte G. Bybee	Lance Corporal	512 Court Street, Portsmouth, Ohio/bartender	
Charles H. Maguire	Corporal	3 West Fifth Street, Portsmouth, Ohio/telegraph operator	

Name	Rank When Mustered Out	Residence/ Occupation	Comment
Joseph C. Bratt	Corporal	459 East Ninth Street, Portsmouth, Ohio/civil engineer	
Harvey N. Will	Corporal	Clerk	
Charles H. Reed	Corporal	Clerk	
Denver Crull	Corporal	Farmer	
George A. Batterson	Corporal	Student	
Clinton M. Searl	Corporal	14 East Ninth Street, Portsmouth, Ohio/law student	
Asbury W. Davidson	Corporal	Shoe cutter	
John L. McMonigle	Corporal	108 Bond Street, Portsmouth, Ohio/produce commission merchant	
Byron D. Shriver	Corporal	Farmer	
William P. Reed	Corporal	34 West Second Street, Portsmouth, Ohio/attorney	
Charles S. Noel IV	Corporal	Clerk	
Floyd E. Thurman	Corporal	Elk Building, Room 12, Portsmouth, Ohio/agent, *Commercial Gazette*	

Name	Rank When Mustered Out	Residence/ Occupation	Comment
Roy M. Mathews	Artificer	Teacher	
Harry W. Donaldson	Artificer	148 East Eighth Street, Portsmouth, Ohio/carpenter	
Fred M. Armstrong	Musician	Clerk	His middle initial may have been "N."
William D. McMonigle	Wagoner	Teamster	
Barry J. Alger	Private	205 East Second Street, Portsmouth, Ohio/worked for architects	
Frank H. Alger	Private	205 East Second Street, Portsmouth, Ohio/worked for architects	
Preston H. Anderson	Private	823 Offnere Street, Portsmouth, Ohio/clerk	
Harry E. Adams	Private	1418 Waller Street, Portsmouth, Ohio/ironworker	
Benjamin L. Andre	Private	Bookkeeper	
Albert M. Barber	Private	320 Gallia Street, Portsmouth, Ohio/shoe worker	
Elton M. Bumgardner	Private	Lumber grader	

Appendix A

Name	Rank When Mustered Out	Residence/ Occupation	Comment
Francis M. Bush	Private	Laborer	
Thomas J. Bush	Private	82 East Front Street, rear building, Portsmouth, Ohio/laborer	
Mathew Bush	Private	Laborer	
Elmer S. Boren	Private	Laborer/ carpenter	
Charles Barr	Private	29 West Second Street, Portsmouth, Ohio/barkeeper	
David P. Bennett	Private	528 Robinson Avenue, Portsmouth, Ohio/shoe worker	
John L. Birmingham	Private	Laborer	
Forest C. Briggs	Private	Stenographer	He died on November 10, 1898.
Ralph W. Calvert	Private	164 East Second Street, Portsmouth, Ohio/shipping clerk	
Milton J. Cooper	Private	Machinist	
William L. Cole	Private	Farmer	
Taswell Chapman	Private	218 Chillicothe Street, Portsmouth, Ohio/shoe worker	

Name	Rank When Mustered Out	Residence/ Occupation	Comment
Vinton A. Cunningham	Private	1304 Summit Street, Portsmouth, Ohio/barber	
Reed M. Davidson	Private	Student	
Louis E. Distel	Private	114 Scioto Street, Portsmouth, Ohio/shoe worker	
Duncan M. Douglas	Private	Clerk	
David C. Davis	Private	Laborer	
Daniel H. Dodge	Private	261 East Sixth Street, Portsmouth, Ohio/shoe cutter and clerk	He died on August 10, 1898, in Puerto Rico.
Mitchell H. Evans	Private	Shoe worker	
Robert M. George	Private	Shoemaker	
John F. Getz	Private	Embalmer	
Ora B. Gilbert	Private	Agent	
Edward B. Hicks	Private	95 East Front Street, Portsmouth, Ohio/shoe worker	
Albert G. Herms	Private	Florist	
John A. Hubert	Private	325 East Tenth Street, Portsmouth, Ohio/member of Company H	

Name	Rank When Mustered Out	Residence/ Occupation	Comment
Charles E. Hood	Private	929 Chillicothe Street, Portsmouth, Ohio/wheel worker	
George E. Hood	Private	Carpenter	
Evan G. Harris	Private	17 West Fourth Street, Portsmouth, Ohio/shoe worker	
David J. Johnson	Private	447 East Fifth Street, rear building, Portsmouth, Ohio/member of Company H	
Samuel E. Johnson	Private	916 Gay Street, Portsmouth, Ohio/painter	
William E. Johnson	Private	32 Thirteenth Street, Portsmouth, Ohio/member of Company H	
Wells Jones	Private	620 East Eighth Street, Portsmouth, Ohio/clerk	
John Wesley Kinney	Private	101 East Second Street, Portsmouth, Ohio/salesman	
Clifford M. Kinney	Private	101 East Second Street, Portsmouth, Ohio/member of Company H and student	

Name	Rank When Mustered Out	Residence/ Occupation	Comment
William H. Kelly	Private	300 Jackson Street, Portsmouth, Ohio/letter carrier	
Isaac Krick	Private	129 East Eighth Street, Portsmouth, Ohio/brakeman	
George T. Mann	Private	Motorman	
William A. Masters	Private	Clerk	
Harry W. Mathiot	Private	916 Gay Street, Portsmouth, Ohio/shoe worker	
James McDaniels	Private	Laborer	
Edward M. McGuire	Private	37 West Ninth Street, Portsmouth, Ohio/ paperhanger	
Emmett K. McKeown	Private	416 Bond Street, Portsmouth, Ohio/ stenographer and clerk	
Alexander R. Mead	Private	238 Gallia Street, Portsmouth, Ohio/carpenter and painter	
Alfred M. Messer	Private	Laborer	
Harry U. Mohl	Private	115 East Fourth Street, Portsmouth, Ohio/shoe worker	

Name	Rank When Mustered Out	Residence/ Occupation	Comment
Charles G. Molster	Private	361 East Front Street, Portsmouth, Ohio/member of Company H	
John E. Monk	Private	140 East Front Street, Portsmouth, Ohio/clerk	
George E. Moore	Private	Laborer	
Henry M. Morrison	Private	Shoemaker	He died on October 26, 1898, and was buried at sea.
Charles S. Noel	Private	Clerk	
Elbert L. Patterson	Private	395 East Eleventh Street, Portsmouth, Ohio/worked for his father's newspaper	He graduated high school in 1897 and died in Puerto Rico on October 16, 1898.
William M. Peebles	Private	Coal engineer	
Joseph A. Redman	Private	Shoemaker	
Edward J. Reinhardt	Private	113 West Seventh Street, Portsmouth, Ohio/tinner	
Adolph G. Reinert	Private	119 Gallia Street, upstairs room, Portsmouth, Ohio/drug clerk	
Kurt Sparka	Private	Columbus, Ohio	He died on October 5, 1898.

Name	Rank When Mustered Out	Residence/ Occupation	Comment
William C. Sturgill	Private	Ironton, Ohio/ teacher	
James F. Stewart	Private	38 West Fourth Street, Portsmouth, Ohio/salesman	
Walter H. Stone	Private	237 Sixth Street, Portsmouth, Ohio/plasterer	
James Skelton	Private	New Boston, Ohio/real estate	
John W. Shela	Private	120 Gallia Street, Portsmouth, Ohio/letter carrier	
John F. Schmitt	Private	423 Bond Street, Portsmouth, Ohio/solicitor	
Mathew W. Thompson	Private	803 Findley Street, Portsmouth, Ohio/insurance	
Charles C. Taylor	Private	332 East Third Street, Portsmouth, Ohio	
William E. Thomas	Private	Laborer	
Joseph Turner	Private	1013 Findley Street, Portsmouth, Ohio/laborer and janitor	
Edgar S. Wells	Private	Clerk	
Charles R. Whitman	Private	Brick worker	

Name	Rank When Mustered Out	Residence/ Occupation	Comment
Arthur R. Welch	Private	814 Washington Street, Portsmouth, Ohio/shoe laster	
Edgar R. Wheeler	Private	120 Gallia Street, Portsmouth, Ohio/shoe worker	
Henry H. Winters	Private	140 East Eighth Street, Portsmouth, Ohio/clerk	
John Youngman	Private	62 East Eleventh Street, Portsmouth, Ohio/clerk	
Edward Zeek	Private	Ironton, Ohio/ engineer	

APPENDIX B

Other Scioto Countians Who Served in the Spanish-American War

Name	Rank/Unit	Residence/Occupation	Comment
Frank G. Allard	Private, Sixth U.S. Infantry	Sciotoville, Ohio	He was wounded in the foot at the Battle of Santiago, Cuba. He died of typhoid on July 18, 1898, while in the hospital.
Arthur P. Bagby	Private, Company M, Fourth Ohio Volunteer Infantry	Portsmouth, Ohio	
Clyde Barber	First Ohio Volunteer Infantry	Portsmouth, Ohio	
Frank J. Batterson	Private, Signal Corps	Sciotoville, Ohio/ electrician	

Name	Rank/Unit	Residence/ Occupation	Comment
John J. Bennett	U.S. Navy		He served on the auxiliary cruiser *Franklin*.
Charles C. Cole	Private, Troop D, First Ohio Cavalry	Portsmouth, Ohio	
Jacob C. Craft	Sergeant	Sugar Grove, Ohio/career military	He served for six enlistments and retired in 1913.
William Cunningham			
Charles J. Darlington	Company H, First Missouri	Lucasville, Ohio	
Alexander B. Davies	Artificer, Company A, Tenth Ohio Volunteer Infantry	Portsmouth, Ohio	
Fairfax Dickey	Third Sergeant, Company B, Fourth Kentucky Volunteer Infantry	Portsmouth, Ohio	
John P. Doyle	Company L, First Florida Volunteer Infantry	Portsmouth, Ohio	
Frank Eakens	U.S. Navy	Sciotoville, Ohio	
Pat Foley	U.S. Marines	Portsmouth, Ohio	He participated in the battle for Guantanamo, Cuba.
George Friend	Pharmacist/U.S. Navy	Portsmouth, Ohio	
John Good Jr.	U.S. Heavy Artillery	Portsmouth, Ohio	
William W. Hadley	Private, Signal Corps	Portsmouth, Ohio/telegrapher	

Appendix B

Name	Rank/Unit	Residence/Occupation	Comment
"Monk" Herder	First West Virginia	Findlay Street, Portsmouth, Ohio/cigar maker	
Jacob T. Hobstetter	Private, First Battalion, Ohio Light Artillery, Battery C	Portsmouth, Ohio	
Franklin D. Hodge	Corporal, Telegraphic Instructor for War Department	Pueblo, Colorado	
Frank Holt	Company D, Sixth U.S. Infantry	Freestone, Ohio	He participated in the Battle of El Caney and San Juan Blockhouse, Cuba.
Chancy Tilden Hughes	Sixth U.S. Cavalry		He participated in the Battle of Santiago, Cuba.
Frank A. Hummel	Private	Scioto County, Ohio	He was mustered in Ironton, Ohio, and discharged in Havana, Cuba.
Andrew B. Jackson	Private, Hospital Corps	Portsmouth, Ohio	
D.W. Jones	Musician, Virginia Infantry	Portsmouth, Ohio/assistant storekeeper, N&W Railroad	
John M. Kennedy	Private	Otway, Ohio	
Wade Kennedy	Third U.S. Infantry	Portsmouth, Ohio	His brother Captain Case Kennedy was involved in the Indian Wars in Minnesota.
Nicholas Kitt Jr.	Private, Company K, Fourth Ohio Volunteer Infantry	Portsmouth, Ohio	

Name	Rank/Unit	Residence/ Occupation	Comment
Burt Kizer	First Colorado	Portsmouth, Ohio/farmer	
Fred Lewis	Sixth U.S. Cavalry	Portsmouth, Ohio	He was on the staff of General William Shafter, the commander of U.S. Army in Cuba.
Al McGlone		Portsmouth, Ohio	He was wounded in the Battle of Santiago, Cuba.
John McQuaide	Private, Company M, Fourth Virginia Infantry	Portsmouth, Ohio	
Joe Merrill	Private, Company B, Fourth Kentucky Volunteer Infantry	Portsmouth, Ohio	
John Mershon	Second U.S. Infantry	Portsmouth, Ohio	
A.P. Osborn	Lieutenant, U.S. Navy	Wheelersburg, Ohio	He served aboard the cruiser *New Orleans*.
John G. Peebles	Private	Portsmouth, Ohio	
John Peebles Jr.	Hospital Corps	Henley, Ohio	He served in Manila.
Walter Reinhard	Bugler, Sixth Massachusetts Infantry	East Seventh Street, Portsmouth, Ohio	
Arthur D. Row	Private	Portsmouth, Ohio	He transferred from Company H, Seventeenth U.S. Infantry, to the Hospital Corps.
Charles Sauffer	Private	Portsmouth, Ohio	He transferred from Company K, Second U.S. Infantry, to the Hospital Corps.

Name	Rank/Unit	Residence/ Occupation	Comment
Jacob H. Smith	Colonel, Second U.S. Infantry.	Portsmouth, Ohio	He was wounded at the Battle of Santiago, Cuba. He was court-martialed for war crimes committed in Philippines and was allowed to retire.
Frank Switalski	Battery H, Ohio Artillery	Portsmouth, Ohio	
A.C. Thompson Jr.	Lieutenant	Portsmouth, Ohio	
Tullius C. Tupper	Chaplain, Field, Staff and Band	Portsmouth, Ohio	
Edward Wiget			
Cliff Wilhelm	Unnamed Texas Regiment	Portsmouth, Ohio	
Clyde H. Williamson	Assistant Engineer, U.S. Navy	Portsmouth, Ohio	He served on the USS *Tecumseh*.

APPENDIX C

GRAVE SITES OF SPANISH-AMERICAN WAR VETERANS BURIED IN SCIOTO COUNTY

(This includes veterans who were not originally from Scioto County but moved there later.)

Name	Date of Birth/ Date of Death	Rank/Unit	Burial Site
Frank G. Allard	1866–July 18, 1898	Private, Company G, Sixth U.S. Infantry	Old Wheelersburg Cemetery, Wheelersburg, Ohio
Albert M. Barber	March 11, 1870– unknown	Private, Company H, Fourth Ohio Volunteer Infantry	Section Robinson-Hill South, Greenlawn Cemetery, Portsmouth, Ohio
James W. Bibbey	1875–1953	Unknown	Friendship Cemetery, Nile Township, Friendship, Ohio
John L. Birmingham	January 21, 1877– unknown	Private, Company H, Fourth Ohio Volunteer Infantry	Section Holy Redeemer, Division D, Greenlawn Cemetery, Portsmouth, Ohio

Name	Date of Birth/ Date of Death	Rank/Unit	Burial Site
Henry B. Bohr	February 28, 1880–August 16, 1947	Private, Third New York Infantry	Section 22, Greenlawn Cemetery, Portsmouth, Ohio
Joseph C. Bratt	Unknown–1941	Corporal, Company H, Fourth Ohio Volunteer Infantry	Greenlawn Cemetery, Portsmouth, Ohio
Forest C. Briggs	July 21, 1872– November 10, 1898	Private, Company H, Fourth Ohio Volunteer Infantry	Greenlawn Cemetery, Portsmouth, Ohio
John W. Burton	February 16, 1875–November 19, 1956	Private, Company B, Sixth Kentucky Infantry	Section D–Harding, Greenlawn Cemetery, Portsmouth, Ohio
Frank M. Bush	December 30, 1873–August 1904	Private, Company H, Fourth Ohio Volunteer Infantry	Old Wheelersburg Cemetery, Wheelersburg, Ohio
William Byers	November 26, 1874–April 22, 1923	Unknown, Company C, Second U.S. Infantry	Section 15, Soldiers' Circle, Greenlawn Cemetery, Portsmouth, Ohio
Taswell Chapman	September 22, 1867–August 21, 1965	Private, Company H, Fourth Ohio Volunteer Infantry	Berea Methodist Church Cemetery, Brush Creek Township, Ohio
George Carroll	April 12, 1968– May 13, 1950	Unknown, Company H, Seventh Ohio Volunteer Infantry	Section 13, Greenlawn Cemetery, Portsmouth, Ohio
James L. Carroll	December 25, 1876–April 11, 1918	Unknown, Company A, Second U.S. Infantry	St. Mary's Section (19), German Catholic Cemetery, Greenlawn Cemetery, Portsmouth, Ohio
Samuel Colburn	March 18, 1875– March 17, 1950	Private, Second Kentucky Infantry	Section 13, Greenlawn Cemetery, Portsmouth, Ohio

Name	Date of Birth/ Date of Death	Rank/Unit	Burial Site
Charles E. Daniels	April 16, 1874– April 5, 1919	Unknown, Company K, First Illinois Cavalry	Section Robinson-Hill South, Greenlawn Cemetery, Portsmouth, Ohio
Lovell Dixon	1875–1937	Unknown, Company G, Fourth Kentucky Infantry	Old Wheelersburg Cemetery, Wheelersburg, Ohio
Daniel H. Dodge	December 24, 1875–August 10, 1898	Private, Company H, Fourth Ohio Volunteer Infantry	Section 17, Greenlawn Cemetery, Portsmouth, Ohio
James F. Donley	1869–1943	Unknown	Section 2, South Webster Cemetery, South Webster, Ohio
Lewis Erwin	Unknown	Unknown, Company K, Second U.S. Infantry	Section D–Veterans, Greenlawn Cemetery, Portsmouth, Ohio
Lloyd Fleming	November 13, 1878–August 20, 1938	Private, Company M, Third Kentucky Infantry	Section F, Greenlawn Cemetery, Portsmouth, Ohio
Kinney P. Funk	September 24, 1875–September 5, 1918	First Lieutenant, Company H, Fourth Ohio Volunteer Infantry	Section 6, Greenlawn Cemetery, Portsmouth, Ohio
George W. Gibbs	1881–1909	Unknown, Company B, Fourth Kentucky Infantry	Section 9, Greenlawn Cemetery, Portsmouth, Ohio
Henry W. Gibbs	Unknown	Unknown, Company B, Fourth Kentucky Infantry	Section D–Veterans, Greenlawn Cemetery, Portsmouth, Ohio
James Gibbs	1871–1912	Unknown, Company B, Fourth Kentucky Infantry	Section 15, Soldiers' Circle, Greenlawn Cemetery, Portsmouth, Ohio

Name	Date of Birth/ Date of Death	Rank/Unit	Burial Site
Ernest Goldfinch	April 16, 1875– June 8, 1946	Unknown, Thirty-First Michigan Infantry	Old Wheelersburg Cemetery, Wheelersburg, Ohio
David Frank Griffith	June 23, 1880– May 22, 1956	Unknown, Company M, Second U.S. Infantry	Pine Grove Cemetery, Fallen Timber Road, Lucasville, Ohio
Daniel H. Heid	April 13, 1880– February 11, 1920	Unknown, Company K, Twenty-Eighth U.S. Infantry	Section H South–H Alley, Greenlawn Cemetery, Portsmouth, Ohio
George Hollingsworth	Unknown	Unknown, Company B, Fourth Kentucky Infantry	Section 22, Greenlawn Cemetery, Portsmouth, Ohio
Charles Huels	Unknown	Unknown, Company H, Sixth U.S. Infantry	Section Holy Redeemer–Division D, Greenlawn Cemetery, Portsmouth, Ohio
David J. Johnson	Unknown	Private, Company H, Ohio Infantry	Section D, Greenlawn Cemetery, Portsmouth, Ohio
Frank A. Keadle	Unknown	Unknown, Company C, Second West Virginia Infantry	Section D–Veterans, Greenlawn Cemetery, Portsmouth, Ohio
Frank Kelley	July 15, 1870– May 1, 1919	Unknown, Company H, Seventh Ohio Volunteer Infantry	Section 3, Greenlawn Cemetery, Portsmouth, Ohio
Clifford M. Kinney	July 18, 1879– June 28, 1956	Private, Company H, Fourth Ohio Volunteer Infantry	Section 6, Greenlawn Cemetery, Portsmouth, Ohio
John Wesley Kinney	July 10, 1877–July 16, 1952	Private, Company H, Fourth Ohio Volunteer Infantry	Section 6, Greenlawn Cemetery, Portsmouth, Ohio

Name	Date of Birth/ Date of Death	Rank/Unit	Burial Site
James C. Kitts	Unknown	Musician, Twelfth U.S. Infantry	Section D–Veterans, Greenlawn Cemetery, Portsmouth, Ohio
George C. Lauder	Unknown	Private, Seventh Ohio Volunteer Infantry	St. Peter's Catholic Cemetery, Wheelersburg, Ohio
Charles E. Lipker	Unknown	Corporal, General Services, Infantry	Old Wheelersburg Cemetery, Wheelersburg, Ohio
Harry W. Mathiott	Unknown	Private, Company H, Fourth Ohio Volunteer Infantry	Section H, North, Greenlawn Cemetery, Portsmouth, Ohio
William C. McGlone	July 30, 1875– May 20, 1958	Private, Company F, Fourth Kentucky Infantry	Bennett Cemetery, Madison Township, Minford, Ohio
Edward McGuire	October 28, 1874–unknown	Unknown, Company A, Fourth Ohio Volunteer Infantry	Section–Holy Redeemer–Division D, Greenlawn Cemetery, Portsmouth, Ohio
Emmett K. McKeown	Unknown	Private, Company H, Fourth Ohio Volunteer Infantry	Section D–Veterans, Greenlawn Cemetery, Portsmouth, Ohio
John N. McLeod	April 26, 1881– unknown	Private, Company B, Second West Virginia Infantry	H South–H Alley, Greenlawn Cemetery, Portsmouth, Ohio
C.B. Moore	Unknown	Unknown, Company H, Fourth Ohio Volunteer Infantry	Old Wheelersburg Cemetery, Wheelersburg, Ohio
Clara M. Moore	1874–1957	Nurse	Section 5, South Webster Cemetery, South Webster, Ohio
William W. Moore	September 4, 1878–December 10, 1959	Musician, Company I, Sixteenth U.S. Infantry (bugler and sharpshooter)	Old Wheelersburg Cemetery, Wheelersburg, Ohio

Name	Date of Birth/ Date of Death	Rank/Unit	Burial Site
Chris E. Moritz	Unknown	Unknown, Company M, Second U.S. Infantry	Lucasville Cemetery, Lucasville, Ohio
Oliver N. Nash	Unknown	Unknown, Battery C, First Battalion Ohio Light Artillery	Greenlawn Cemetery, Portsmouth, Ohio
Charles Soloman Noel IV	October 25, 1872–January 9, 1963	Corporal, Company H, Fourth Ohio Volunteer Infantry	Section 16, Greenlawn Cemetery, Portsmouth, Ohio
John W. Powers	1874–1899	Unknown, Company F, Sixteenth U.S. Infantry	Old Wheelersburg Cemetery, Wheelersburg, Ohio
Charles Pratt	1864–1938	Unknown, Second U.S. Infantry	Section 22, Greenlawn Cemetery, Portsmouth, Ohio
Adolph G. Reinert	March 20, 1876– November 23, 1958	Private, Company H, Fourth Ohio Volunteer Infantry	Section 13, Greenlawn Cemetery, Portsmouth, Ohio
Walter E. Reinhard	1879–1937	Private, Band, Sixth Massachusetts Infantry	Section 14, Greenlawn Cemetery, Portsmouth, Ohio
Washington Riggs	September 18, 1870–April 11, 1956	Private, Company M, Third Kentucky Infantry	Section 13, Greenlawn Cemetery, Portsmouth, Ohio
George Lewis Sartain	October 16, 1879–January 7, 1932	Unknown, Troop M, Twelfth U.S. Cavalry	Old Wheelersburg Cemetery, Wheelersburg, Ohio
Tilden F. Skaggs	October 12, 1876–November 29, 1925	Private, Company G, A [sic] Regiment U.S.	Section D–Harding, Greenlawn Cemetery, Portsmouth, Ohio

Name	Date of Birth/ Date of Death	Rank/Unit	Burial Site
James W. Smith	May 21, 1871– February 9, 1944	Captain, Company H, Fourth Ohio Volunteer Infantry	Section D–Veterans, Greenlawn Cemetery, Portsmouth, Ohio
James Stanley	March 25, 1883– December 6, 1965	Private, Seventeenth U.S. Infantry	Old Wheelersburg Cemetery, Wheelersburg, Ohio
Ernest Stockham	July 13, 1877– February 2, 1951	Private, Company B, Fourth Kentucky Infantry	Section Evergreen Division, Greenlawn Cemetery, Portsmouth, Ohio
Willard Thomas	Unknown	Unknown, Hospital Corps	Section D–Veterans, Greenlawn Cemetery, Portsmouth, Ohio
Joseph Turner	Unknown	Private, Company H, Fourth Ohio Volunteer Infantry	Section B, Greenlawn Cemetery, Portsmouth, Ohio
James A. Waddell	February 22, 1863–March 6, 1931	Unknown, Company A, Sixth Indiana Infantry	Section D–Veterans, Greenlawn Cemetery, Portsmouth, Ohio
Robert Waddell Sr.	January 2, 1877– February 2, 1968	Unknown, Company L, Second U.S. Infantry	Junior Furnace Cemetery, Green Township, Franklin Furnace, Ohio
William E. Warner	October 21, 1876–January 29, 1963	Master Sergeant, Ohio Quartermaster Corps	Section Holy Redeemer–Division G, Greenlawn Cemetery, Portsmouth, Ohio
Edgar S. Wells	1871–1936	Private, Company H, Fourth Ohio Volunteer Infantry	Section 16, Greenlawn Cemetery, Portsmouth, Ohio
Charles R. Welty	January 25, 1875– May 12, 1965	Corporal, Company G, Thirty-Eighth U.S. Infantry	Friendship Cemetery, Nile Township, Friendship, Ohio

Name	Date of Birth/ Date of Death	Rank/Unit	Burial Site
Jacob A. Willis	March 25, 1873–May 9, 1939	Private, Company A, Fourth Kentucky Infantry	Section 4, South Webster Cemetery, South Webster, Ohio
Robert Wheeler	November 31, 1878–January 26, 1966	Private, Company L, Second U.S. Infantry	Lucasville Cemetery, Lucasville, Ohio
Ernest Withrow	Unknown	Unknown, Troop B, First Kentucky Cavalry	Section D–Veterans, Greenlawn Cemetery, Portsmouth, Ohio
John Youngman	1881–1922	Private, Company H, Fourth Ohio Volunteer Infantry	Section Evergreen Division D, Greenlawn Cemetery, Portsmouth, Ohio

NOTES

Preface

1. Jacob S. Coxey was from Massillon, Ohio. He had six children. One of his sons was named Legal Tender Coxey.
2. A quote in a letter (July 27, 1898) to Theodore Roosevelt from the United States secretary of state John Hay: "It has been a splendid little war, begun with the highest motives, carried on with magnificent intelligence and spirit, favored by that fortune which loves the brave."
3. Company H was part of the Fourteenth Infantry, Ohio National Guard. When mustered into federal service, its designation became the Fourth Ohio Volunteer Infantry.

Chapter 1

4. Recently, the Ye Olde Lantern restaurant, which had been vacant, has undergone renovation. At the time of the Spanish-American War, the Enos Reed Pharmacy, which was in the same location, was replaced by Wurster Brothers Pharmacy. The *Portsmouth Blade* newspaper office was on the second floor.

Chapter 2

5. Two navy courts of inquiry, the Sampson Board of 1898 and the Vreeland Board of 1911, concluded that the sinking of the USS *Maine* was due to the detonation of a Spanish mine triggering an explosion in the ship's magazine. Neither investigation concluded that the mine was intentionally planted for the purpose of destroying the ship, but they did hold that Spain was responsible under international law for failing to protect foreign shipping in its harbor. Sixty years later, Admiral Hyman Rickover, USN, concluded that a fire in the *Maine*'s forward coal bunker caused the explosion and not an external source. On the one-hundred-year anniversary of the *Maine*'s destruction, National Geographic commissioned a study utilizing the aid of computer models. It asserted that "it appears more probable" that a mine was the cause of the sinking. *National Geographic* 193, no. 2 (February 1998): 92. Finally, it is the position of the Naval History and Heritage Command that "evidence of a mine remains thin."

Chapter 3

6. Hearst denied making this statement. Nevertheless, through his newspaper, the *New York Journal*, and in his sensationalistic reporting style, he constantly urged U.S. intervention and depicted Spanish authorities as brutal monsters.

Chapter 4

7. In a time when labor strikes often became violent, it was not uncommon for state governments to mobilize national guard units to keep the peace or suppress the strikes. The campaign ribbons on the flag staff of the Fourteenth Infantry, Ohio National Guard, was for service rendered in the preceding two decades.
8. In an effort to boost participation in drill, an absent member was fined thirty cents.
9. Captain Milstead of the local Bailey Post of the Grand Army of the Republic was supposed to give a speech, but the *Portsmouth Blade* reported that "unforeseen changes in the program prevented him from doing so."

However, the newspaper felt it was worthy to print the entire speech in its next edition. It included such noble phrasing as:

> *The enemy we fought* [the Confederacy] *were American citizens, nearly, if not quite our equal, both in manhood and Christianity.... The foe that confronts you, the hated Spanish, is wholly devoid of manhood and humanity.... You are leaving at home good Christian mothers, wives, sisters and sweethearts, who, on bended knees and uplifted faces, will send to the throne of grace their daily prayers for your protection, success and safe return home. Should temptations of an evil nature ever surround you, remember the loved ones at home who are waiting for a good report from you.*

10. In 1853, Tracy Park was given to the city of Portsmouth by Francis Campbell in honor of his attorney, Samuel M Tracy. John R.T. Barnes, the first Scioto County soldier to die in the Civil War, is represented on a forty-foot monument in the center of the park, which was dedicated in 1879. The popular park, which is located in the center of the city, has served as a gathering place for recreation, rallies, musical events, casual get-togethers and religious meetings.

Chapter 5

11. An artificer in the United States military of the era was a soldier responsible for the maintenance of a unit's equipment (basically a mechanic and repair person). Usually, one artificer was provided in each infantry company, cavalry troop and artillery battery.
12. Frederick Dent Grant was the eldest son of Ulysses S. Grant, the commander of the Union army during the Civil War and the eighteenth president of the United States. At the outbreak of the Spanish-American War, Frederick was commissioned as a colonel and was soon promoted to brigadier general of volunteers.

Chapter 6

13. Both the *Portsmouth Daily Times* and *Portsmouth Blade* were delivered to Company H during their absence.

14. Wenonah Stevens Abbott (1865–1950) was an American journalist, writer and lecturer who was frequently assailed and threatened by the Ku Klux Klan for her reporting on the plight of African Americans.
15. It's no wonder that the entire Caribbean undertaking was described as "the most over-reported military operation" prior to the United States' invasion of Grenada in 1982. Nofi, *Spanish-American War.*

Chapter 7

16. Porto Rico ("rich port") was named by the Spanish and means after gold was discovered. Until 1932, the island was called Porto Rico. Since 1917, Puerto Ricans have been citizens of the United States.
17. Young Funk was named after the Ohio secretary of state at the time, Charles Kinney, a Scioto County native and close friend of his father, attorney Theodore Funk.
18. The officer candidate medical examination of Kinney P. Funk revealed that he had a severe case of gonorrhea and varicose veins. Interestingly, the examiner concluded his condition would not interfere with his duties as an officer.
19. After arriving in Puerto Rico, Private Funk caught the next passage to the United States, where he began a campaign against Colonel Coit's decision to strip him of his commission, eventually filing a lawsuit that was dismissed. Five days after Company H returned to Columbus, Ohio, on November 6, 1898, Governor Bushnell promoted Funk second lieutenant.
20. Camp Hains was named after Brigadier General Peter C. Hains, who was in command of the Second Brigade of the First Division of the First Corps. The Second Brigade included the Fourth Ohio Volunteer Infantry.

Chapter 8

21. The Krag-Jorgensen rifle replaced the Springfield. A major advantage was that the Krag-Jorgensen used smokeless powder rather than black powder, which betrayed the position of the shooter. Company H was issued Krag-Jorgensen rifles while on board the *St. Paul*, which was steaming toward Puerto Rico.

Chapter 9

22. The *St. Paul* was a former passenger liner chartered by the United States Navy. It was outfitted with guns and used as a cruiser during the war. Afterward, it was returned to its owner until it was chartered again in 1917 for service in World War I. It was eventually returned to private ownership and was scrapped in 1923.
23. A letter from Gunner's Mate William J. Bennett to Private William Karg, dated September 27, 1898.
24. The Studebaker Company started building wagons for the Union army during the Civil War. During the Spanish-American War, it supplied five hundred wagons for the effort (www.historynet.com). The Budweiser beer wagon is a Studebaker.
25. Frank Alger's letter home.
26. First published in 1881, the *Century* began as a Christian magazine but gradually began to speak to a more general educated audience as it developed into the largest periodical in the country. It was last published in 1930.

Chapter 10

27. Most likely Private Vinton A. Cunningham.
28. Nelson Appleton Miles (August 8, 1839–May 15, 1925) was an American military general who served in the American Civil War, the American Indian Wars and the Spanish-American War.
29. Launched as the SS *City of Chester* in 1873, it was renamed SS *Sedgwick* when the U.S. Navy took possession of it for use as a transport ship during the war. Later, it was sold to Italian owners, who scrapped it in 1907.

Chapter 11

30. Spanish rule had been brutal, so the populace eagerly welcomed the American invasion. The American command went out of its way to maintain and foster good relations with the locals. When it was learned that an American soldier had defrauded a restaurant by paying with Confederate money, he was court-martialed and sentenced to thirteen

months in a federal penitentiary. The attempt by the United States to have Spain release political prisoners held in Spain encouraged amity of Puerto Ricans to the United States.

31. His name does not appear on any official roster or any muster-in/muster-out rolls for Company H, but he was mentioned in the *Daily Times* on October 6, 1898, as a Company H member.

32. Sergeant Major Creager reprinted in his book, *The Fourteenth Ohio National Guard—The Fourth Ohio Volunteer Infantry*, a statement given by an officer of the Fourth concerning the treatment his brother received in the hospital. It read, in part:

> *Sick men were loaded and unloaded several times from the ambulance. The men were finally moved, while it was raining, and that evening there came to me an intimation that they were not being properly taken care of. I immediately went to the hospital, where my eyes were greeted with a sight I hope never to be witnessed again. Men in all stages of fever and other kinds of sickness were lying on the ground with nothing to lie upon save their own blankets, and a large portion of the men were not under even a tent, but were lying beneath a fly, where the rain was dripping in upon them, and for over a week the men had nothing to eat except regular army rations, unless some kind hearted comrade would spend some of his meager salary for food for his friend.*

33. Musicant, *Empire by Default*.

34. The official roster spells his name "Kurt Sparka." In other documents, it is spelled "Kurt Sparks."

35. They were Sisters Mary Brendam and Mary Edberga, Dr. Emma O. Jones and a Mrs. Taylor. At a time when female physicians were a rarity, Dr. Jones was esteemed enough in her field to be elected president of the Practitioners' Society in 1911. She graduated from Northwestern University Women's Medical School in 1890. She had a practice at 380 East Long Street and later at 697 East Broad Street in Columbus, Ohio.

Chapter 12

36. Corporal Searl's father was Fernando Cortez Searl (July 18, 1825–June 26, 1904). He was the first probate judge in Scioto County, Ohio, as well

NOTE TO PAGE 87

as a poet. He honored his son's request by composing the following poem, which was published posthumously by his family in *Collected Poems of Fernando C. Searl* (1930).

The storm had passed its fury, and the sun's malignant glare,
Had changed the seething cess-pools into vapors of the air;
Beneath the bloom and verdure, hid the demon of despair.
Here the Life from Death was springing, and the earth with verdure dressed,
And the tropic bird was singing to her fledging in the nest:
But the soldier from Ohio was fitful with unrest.

He was lonely in the Island, strange scenes around him lay;
And the lovely haunts of childhood, grew dim and far away,
When a message from his homeland said, "Your papa's on the way."

"Papa's coming, Papa's coming," is all the soldier said.
If the lingering, fading memory of the dying may be read,
He was home among his kindred, as he slept upon his bed.

For in his dying memory, his fancy wandered north,
To feel the cooling breezes that gambol in the north,
To drink from crystal fountains, that were gushing in the north.

He talked a while with papa, when office hours were done,
He soothed the weeping mother, who was grieving for her son,
Who came not at her bidding, though the victory was won.

But the waiting maid beside him, as she watched the ebb and flow
Of his life's o'er burthened current, saw the hectic come and go;
And the eyes grow dim and wander, as the tide of life ran low.

"Papa's coming, papa's coming," seemed to whisper from his bed,
"And his arm is underneath me, and his hand is on my head,
He will bear me home to mother, when he finds that I am dead."

But the waiting maid beside him who, her faithful vigil kept,
Saw the angles gather 'round him as he passed away and slept,
She thought of his home and kindred, and she bowed her head and wept.

37. The last paragraph in Charles Dickens's *David Copperfield* reads:

> *And now, as I close my task, subduing my desire to linger yet, these faces fade away. But one face, shining on me like a Heavenly light by which I see all other objects, is above them and beyond them all. And that remains.*
>   *I turn my head, and see it, in its beautiful serenity, beside me.*
>   *My lamp burns low, and I have written far into the night; but the dear presence, without which I were nothing, bears me company.*
>   *O Agnes, O my soul, so may thy face be by me when I close my life indeed; so may I, when realities are melting from me, like the shadows which I now dismiss, still find thee near me, pointing upward!*

Chapter 13

38. In an effort to stop the spread of disease, the army instituted a program of quarantining afflicted soldiers. A five-thousand-acre site at Montauk Point at the northern end of Long Island, New York, named Camp Wikoff was remote enough from population centers for effective quarantine. At first, the army was not convinced the problem of disease was a matter of urgency and took its time constructing adequate facilities and transferring soldiers to the camp. Commanders in the field, however, were able to convince officials in Washington that conditions were dire and needed immediate intervention. Soldiers from the Cuban Campaign were transferred there, but due to the lack of shelter and adequate rations, conditions there became unhealthy. Soldiers died at Camp Wikoff, where they had been sent to recover. Fortunately, Company H avoided Camp Wikoff; otherwise, its casualty list of five would have undoubtedly grown.

Chapter 14

39. Probably located at 11 West Second Street.
40. Probably located at 16–18 East Fourth Street.
41. No relation to Dr. Hector Soto of the Philippines, who practiced medicine in Portsmouth for thirty-nine years. He died on November 29, 2012.

Chapter 15

42. In 1902, he was the first in Scioto County to own an automobile, a two-cylinder Lane Steamer capable of reaching fifteen miles per hour.
43. In the mid-1920s, Charles H. Noel IV became the Scioto County engineer. He resigned from the engineer's office in 1929 and purchased 144 acres in Pike County. His property was taken by the federal government in 1952 for the construction of the Atomic Energy Commission's uranium enrichment plant. Preston H. Anderson moved to San Francisco and opened a dry goods store.
44. The grave marker of James F. Donley (1869–1943) states he served in Cuba, Porto Rico and the Philippine Islands. He is buried in Section 2, South Webster Cemetery, South Webster, Ohio.

Conclusion

45. Clifford M. Kinney of Company H and William E. Warner of the Quartermaster Corps, veterans of the Spanish-American War who also served in World War I.

BIBLIOGRAPHY

Websites

HistoryNet. www.historynet.com

Naval History and Heritage Command. "The Destruction of the USS Maine." www.history.naval.mil.

Spanish-American War Centennial Website. "The American Army Moves on Puerto Rico." www.spanamwar.com.

———. "A Brief History of the 4th Ohio Volunteer Infantry." www.spanamwar.com.

Books

Cosmas, Graham A. *An Army for Empire: The United States in the Spanish-American War.* 2nd printing, Shippensburg, PA: White Mane Publishing Company Inc., 1994.

Creager, Sergeant Major Charles E. *The Fourteenth Ohio National Guard—The Fourth Ohio Volunteer Infantry.* Columbus, OH: Landon Printing & Publishing Company, 1899.

Dyal, Donald H. *Historical Dictionary of the Spanish-American War.* Westport, CT: Greenwood Press, 1996.

Lodge, Henry Cabot. *The War with Spain.* New York: Harper & Brothers Publishers, 1902.

Miller, Stuart Creighton. "Smith, Jacob Hurd (1840–1918)." In *The War of 1898 and U.S. Interventions 1898–1934: An Encyclopedia.* Edited by Benjamin R. Beede. New York: Garland Publishing Inc., 1994.

Musicant, Ivan. *Empire by Default: The Spanish-American War and the Dawn of the American Century.* New York: Henry Holt and Company, 1998.

Nofi, Albert A. *The Spanish-American War, 1898.* Conshohocken, PA: Combined Books Inc., 1996.

O'Tool, G.J.A. *The Spanish War: An American Epic—1898.* New York: W.W. Horton & Company Inc., 1984.

Perez, Louis A., Jr. *The War of 1898.* Chapel Hill: University of North Carolina Press, 1998.

Searl, Fernando Cortez. *The Collected Poems of Fernando C. Searl.* Published posthumously by his family. Portsmouth, OH: Spahr & Glenn Company, 1930.

Trask, David F. *The War with Spain in 1898.* New York: Free Press, a division of Simon and Schuster Inc., 1981.

Traxel, David. *1898: The Tumultuous Year of Victory, Invention, Internal Strife, and Industrial Expansion that Saw the Birth of the American Century.* New York: Alfred A. Knopf Inc., 1998.

Periodicals

Allen, Thomas B. "Remember the *Maine.*" *National Geographic* 193, no. 2 (February 1998): 93–111.

Albums, Photos, Drawings, Paintings

King, W. Nephew, Lieutenant, U.S. Navy, comp. *The Story of the War of 1898/The Story of the Spanish-American War and the Revolt in the Philippines.* New York: Peter Fenelon Collier & Son, 1900.

Wright, Marcus J., General. *Leslie's Official History of the Spanish-American War.* Washington, D.C.: War Records Office, 1899.

Newspapers

Boston Sunday Globe. July 17, 1898.
Daily Times (Portsmouth, OH). Various dates.
Dayton Evening Herald (Dayton, OH). July 2, 1898.
Examiner (San Francisco, CA). July 1, 1898.
New York Times. May 2, 1898.
Philadelphia Inquirer. June 25, 1898.
Portsmouth Blade (Portsmouth, OH). Various dates.
Portsmouth Daily Times (Portsmouth, OH). Various dates.
Sun (Baltimore, MD). July 4, 1898.
Washington Times. June 23, 1898.

Libraries

National Archives (Washington, D.C.)
Ohio History Connection (Columbus, OH)
Portsmouth Public Library (Portsmouth, OH)

Other

Diaries of Captain William Moore and that of his daughter Louisiana (1898). Located in the Local History section of the Portsmouth Public Library, 1220 Gallia Street, Portsmouth, Ohio, 45662.
Sons of Spanish-American War Veterans 2018 Yearbook. Vol. 10 (Yearbook Volume 3). Eanes Group, Crewe, Virginia, 2018.

INDEX

ABOUT THE AUTHOR

John McHenry is an attorney with an abiding interest in history. While carousing through old newspapers at the local public library, he came upon a reference to Company H from Portsmouth, Ohio, that participated in the invasion of Puerto Rice during the 1898 Spanish-American War. He knew then that there was a story to tell about soldiers from Portsmouth and Scioto County in general that had been all but lost. Scioto County rallied to the call to arms and in its small way joined in the temper of the time to free oppressed Cubans from the yoke of Spanish rule. Not all returned home.

Mr. McHenry lives in South Webster, Ohio, with his wife, Mary, and their eleven chickens and two beehives. A plan to acquire goats is in the works. Ten percent of his net proceeds will be donated to the Scioto County Heritage Museum.

Visit us at
www.historypress.com

www.ingramcontent.com/pod-product-compliance
Lightning Source LLC
Chambersburg PA
CBHW070926150426
42812CB00049B/1512